Southern Living

ideas for great
TILE

DESIGNER: CHARLOTTE TAYLOR

Oxmoor House®

Southern Living® Ideas for Great Tile was adapted from a book by the same title published by Sunset Books.

Book Editor
Scott Atkinson

Developmental Editor
Linda J. Selden

Consulting Editor
Jane Horn

Copy Editor
Marcia Williamson

Editorial Coordinators
Bradford Kachelhofer, Vicki Weathers

Design
Barbara Vick

Principal Photographer
Philip Harvey

Photo Director
JoAnn Masaoka Van Atta

Production Coordinator
Patricia S. Williams

Special Contributors
Linda Bouchard, Bridget Biscotti Bradley, Barbara Brown, Tishana Peebles, Jean Warboy

Our appreciation to the staff of *Southern Living* magazine for their contributions to this book.

ISBN 0-376-09077-4
Library of Congress Catalog Card Number: 99-65016
Printed in the United States

Cover design by James Boone and Vasken Guiragossian. Photography by Philip Harvey. Photo direction by JoAnn Masaoka Van Atta. Interior designer: Janna Lund Rodgers. Builder: Phillip Blois.

A renaissance in tile

Given the explosion of interest in tile styles, both new and classic, we felt that the time was right for an idea book devoted to this beautiful and versatile material.

In these pages you'll find scores of colorful, inspiring tile installations, an introduction to planning and design basics, a helpful glossary of tile terms, and tips for shopping the showrooms. All this should help you analyze your own needs and tailor a beautiful tile solution.

Many individuals and firms were expert resources for us in planning this book. We're particularly indebted to Lynne B. Roe and to Joseph A. Taylor of the Tile Heritage Foundation for valuable help. Chugrad McAndrews spent many hours ably assisting with location photography.

We'd also like to thank Alchemie Ceramic Studio; ASN Natural Stone; Country Floors; Fireclay Tile; Galleria Tile; Oceanside Glasstile; Buddy Rhodes Studio; ANN SACKS Tile & Stone; Diane Swift; and Tile Visions. Credits for specific product shots are listed on page 112.

TILE ARTISANS: AHMED AGRAMA & TAMARA HARRIS

contents

miles and miles of tiles

MADE FROM earth, water, fire—and, to stretch a point, some air, too—no building material is more elemental than ceramic tile. The earliest versions were simply hand-formed slabs of clay left to bake in the sun. Then, someone must have noticed that clay—perhaps some used to line a primitive oven—was tougher and more water-resistant if baked, or fired, at higher temperatures. And adding wet pigment to the surface of the clay before firing opened up an immense world of ornamental possibilities.

The history of decorative tile goes back at least 6,000 years, to the Egyptians, who used glazed bricks to adorn their houses and temples. Aspects of today's tile designs began with the emergence of metallic glazes in the Islamic world during the eighth and ninth centuries, and develop through Mesopotamia and Persia, Byzantium, and on to the encaustic tiles used in English cathedrals in the 1200s. The trail leads to Moorish architectural and garden ornament in Spain, and to Italy, where in the 16th century the tradition of painted majolica tiles was born. In the 18th century, the Dutch city of Delft innovated the production—much exported—of quaint blue-and-white-glazed earthenware, still popular today. Tile experimentation doubled back to England during the Victorian period, with the development of nature-inspired transfer patterns.

ARCHITECT: ROBERT WYLIE

The early 20th century produced an American tile zenith, with a cornucopia of Arts and Crafts, Art Deco, Hispanic, and other vibrant design statements. Sadly, during the Depression most of these tile makers folded up shop—but, as we'll see, not for good.

What a long way to today's renaissance, abounding in new decorative wall and floor tiles, borders, relief trim, and hand-painted pieces. The proliferation of art tiles—both new designs and period reproductions—is especially inspiring. Some artisans have dedicated themselves to the styles and glazes of the early 1900s heyday; other firms, both large and small, offer fresh, original creations. Imported tiles from Europe and South America are plentiful. Mosaics are making a definite comeback, both custom art pieces and factory-mounted versions. Classics from the past are inspiring a growing interest in tiles as collectibles.

At the same time, new cutting techniques and sealers have made natural stone tiles affordable as well as elegant. The tile market is also welcoming newcomers in glass and concrete. With all these options, you can use tile to decorate any house or garden area in practically any style you can imagine.

The book before you takes a three-phase tour of today's tile choices. We begin with planning, surveying those places where tile can flourish, and examining basic design principles, including consideration of style, color, pattern, and size. Next, we present an extensive, room-by-room gallery of up-to-the-minute tile ideas illustrated in brilliant color photos. We finish with a glossary of representative tile types and terms, giving you a leg up when you visit the showroom or home center. Read straight through the book for a complete survey, or detour as your fancy dictates.

If you're ready to join our tour, simply turn the page.

A PLANNING PRIMER

GIVEN the vast range of beautiful tiles available today, it's safe to say that you'll have no problem finding one that pleases your eye. But when visiting showrooms, it's also important to think about use-appropriateness, overall style, and, of course, your budget. **THIS CHAPTER** is your design workbook. We begin by surveying the many options, review style and design principles, and finish up with some shopping tips. It's both fun and free to brainstorm, and that's an integral part of the planning process. Then consider the details like color, pattern, and scale, juggling them with weightier concerns like maintenance and cost. Thinking of tiling it yourself? For an overview of materials and techniques, see page 29. If you need additional help with planning or installation, we point you toward the professionals who can lend a hand. **FOR FURTHER** inspiration, you'll find plenty of colorful photos of successful installations in "Great Tile Ideas," beginning on page 31. And for a closer look at tile types, see "A Shopper's Guide" on pages 91–111.

exploring your options

TILE LEADS *a double life: on the one hand, it's an amazingly versatile design tool; on the other, it provides hardworking surfaces that give watertight protection where needed. In planning, you explore both of these aspects, then bring them together. Have fun with the colorful, creative design possibilities, but choose the tile type that's most practical for your purpose.*

DESIGN: TAYLOR WOODROW

Where does tile go?

Once upon a time, the use of ceramic tile in the typical American home was reserved for bathrooms and, occasionally, formal entry halls. Now, however, tile has spread into kitchens, living spaces, and outdoor areas, too. No wonder its surge in popularity. Aside from its visual appeal, it is durable, colorfast, easy to maintain, and non-allergenic. And recent diamond-saw technology has made stone tiles nearly as available and affordable as ceramic.

FLOORS. Tile is a natural for floors, as long as it's slip resistant. In entryways, halls, and other heavy-traffic corridors, tile remains rigid and colorfast. An onslaught of wet galoshes or the muddy paws of a family pet will do it no harm. In the kitchen or bathroom, tile provides excellent protection against drips and spills. Cleaning requires merely a damp mop with a soapless detergent.

Tiled flooring makes a strong decorative statement. Depending on the style you choose, you can create any atmosphere—from formal elegance to rustic earthiness. You can link and visually expand spaces by extending a tile floor from entry to living room, and then right out onto the patio.

WALLS. Any wall that might be sprayed or splashed with water is an obvious candidate for glazed ceramic tile. But don't limit tile to areas that get wet. A wainscot or accent of tile in a living room, dining room, or home office makes a neatly tailored backdrop for furnishings, plants, or a freestanding fireplace.

TUBS AND SHOWERS. Around bathroom fixtures, tiled surfaces are waterproof and easy to keep clean of splashes and soap film. Glazed

wall tiles are most familiar, but mosaics shine here, too: they're tough, handsome, and shed water.

COUNTERTOPS. Ideal as a working surface near the kitchen sink and stove, most tile is unaffected by a sharp knife or hot pan. And if you use an appropriate grout (see page 29), grease and food spots wipe right off. Tile makes a decorative but functional surface for any bathroom vanity, eating counter, or wet bar.

BACKSPLASHES. The part of the wall exposed above kitchen and bathroom counters, this eye-level surface is a great place to focus decorative tile effects. Glazing brings water protection and easy cleanup to these spaces, too.

Classic kitchen countertop and backsplash (above) are lined with handpainted Portuguese tiles. A modernistic version (left) teams staggered wall tiles with candy-colored glass dots. Slate floor tiles (facing page) are framed by limestone strips and tiny glass mosaics.

*An outdoor wall
niche is lined with
colorful, Moroccan-
style tile; note how
artfully the curved
wall planes come
together at the top.*

FIREPLACES. Because most ceramic tile is baked at a high temperature, it is unaffected by heat. Consider using tile on the outside face, mantel, or hearth of a fireplace. Even a single row of blue-and-white Delft or earth-toned Arts and Crafts tiles can add character.

STAIRS. Constant traffic wears down the treads of stairs and steps. Surfacing them with tile will protect them for years. For stair treads, be sure to use slip-resistant tiles or tiles with raised edges. For a simple brightening effect, trim the risers with colorful accent tiles. This will also make steps more visible in dim light.

LANDSCAPE ARCHITECT: JEFF STONE ASSOCIATES OF LA JOLLA

ARCHITECT AND INTERIOR DESIGNER: STEPHEN W. SANBORN

*Marble tiles, custom-
cut and arranged in
bold black-and-white
geometrics, face this
living-room fireplace.*

TILE ARTISAN: MARLO BARTELS STUDIO OF LAGUNA BEACH

BUILDER: SALVADOR RODRIGUEZ. TILE: OCEANSIDE GLASSTILE

DECORATIVE BORDERS. Whether set edge-to-edge or spaced apart, tiles make beautiful frames for doors or windows. Consider tiled crown and base moldings, too.

FURNISHINGS. Adding a tile top can give new life to an old table. And why not tile the bases of window seats and built-in benches?

SHELVES AND NICHES. Not only do built-in display shelves, sills, jambs, and greenhouse windows provide many handy horizontal surfaces to decorate, they're also easier to clean when tiled.

SOLARIUMS. Both stone and ceramic tiles are naturals for sunrooms. The clay body's thermal mass retains solar heat in winter, and its firm face is undamaged by plant waterings.

OUTDOORS. Patios and pools are tried-and-true locations for tile. But what about decorative wall fountains, built-in benches, fireplace surrounds, garden walls, and outdoor kitchens?

COLLECTIBLES. Art tiles, especially antiques, are currently in vogue as collectibles. Show off their charm by setting some above a picture rail. Or hang them like paintings.

Outdoor trim tile adorns both an entry gate (top) *and on a poolside fountain* (above right). *The gate insert features jigsaw-shaped tiles and a cast center medallion; the pool edging shimmers with iridescent glass. Stair risers* (right) *are dressed up with Spanish relief tiles, which also wrap around the outside wall. Note the unique, curved trim tiles.*

ARCHITECT: REMICK ASSOCIATES ARCHITECTS-BUILDERS, INC. TILE: STONELIGHT TILE COMPANY

Tile types

Not all tile is created equal. Instead, tiles are characterized according to how they're made and what they're for.

Ceramic tile is either glazed or unglazed. A glaze is a hard finish, usually incorporating a color, that is applied to the surface of the hardened clay body and then, most often, refired one or more additional times. (For more tile-making details, see page 15.) A glaze can have a high gloss, a matte finish, or a dull, pebbly texture.

Unglazed tiles do not have a baked-on finish. The colors you see—commonly earth tones, ranging from yellow-beige to dark red to deep brown—are either from the natural clay itself or from pigments added prior to forming and baking. This color is consistent throughout the body of the tile, whereas glazed tile has color only on the surface.

Clean, simple diamond accents are formed from blue glass mosaics; they're embedded in a plastered backsplash above the kitchen range.

■ **GLAZED WALL TILES** are available in a tremendous variety of colors and designs. Applied to vertical surfaces, these tiles are lighter and thinner than floor tiles. Because they don't need to be particularly strong or slip resistant, they offer many decorative options.

DESIGN: TAYLOR WOODROW

■ **FLOOR TILES** are larger, thicker, and more durable than wall tiles. They come as squares, rectangles, hexagons, and octagons, as well as in interlocking curved shapes, such as Moorish and ogee. Floor tiles are available glazed or unglazed. Unglazed tiles tend to be less slippery and to show wear less easily, since the coloration permeates the tile body. Beware, though: these tiles are more porous and can be tougher to keep clean.

■ **MOSAICS,** used for both walls and floors, are generally small—typically 1 or 2 inches square. Most mosaics come premounted on a mesh backing, ready to install. In custom mosaic art installations, however, the craftsman creates a whimsical, one-of-a-kind composition from broken tiles, glass shards, fragments of china plates and cups, stones, pebbles, bits of mirror, and even marbles.

■ **TRIM AND BORDER TILES** are designed to finish off edges, form coves, and turn inside and outside corners. Use them to break up expanses or serve as transitions between tile patterns or colors, or where the tile meets another surface. You'll also find countertop trim tiles that allow you to tile smoothly around sinks, along counter edges, or below a backsplash.

■ **ART TILES** are created in custom shapes, often glazed with interestingly varied colors and adorned with painted or relief-formed designs. Handpainted tiles, created for tile shops by local artists, offer decorative designs such as flowers, trees, and animals. Using even a few of these beautiful (and expensive) pieces can produce great visual impact when you set them as individual accents in a backsplash wall or countertop. On the other hand, entire scenes, such as a basket of flowers or a group of swimming fish, can be painted on a group of tiles, taken to the site, and reassembled there.

■ **STONE, GLASS, AND CONCRETE TILES** are other vibrant options that can be used in many of the same ways as ceramic. Full information on all these tile types is provided in "A Shopper's Guide," beginning on page 91.

Narrowing the field

You can use tile anywhere in the house where you want durability, beauty, water protection, a bit of flash, or a nod to a period style. But it's best to review the following considerations before you visit the showrooms, where you might be overwhelmed by the options.

MOISTURE RESISTANCE. One key factor when choosing a tile is how easily it absorbs water. Generally speaking, tiles that are fired at higher temperatures for longer times are denser, making them both watertight and resistant to stains.

The most watertight tiles, usually those made from glass and porcelain, are called "impervious," meaning they absorb less than 0.5% moisture. Tiles classified as "vitreous" are the next in line, absorbing 0.5 to 3%, and "semivitreous" tiles absorb 3 to 7%. Soft-bodied "nonvitreous" tiles, such as glazed wall tiles, art tiles, and terra-cotta, absorb 7% or more, and even when treated with a sealer are only partially water resistant. So why do people choose them? Because they're among the most beautiful tiles of all.

High-gloss field tiles, art tile accents, borders, and trim combine to form a shower surround that's both water resistant and a real eye-opener in the morning.

DESIGN: TAYLOR WOODROW

DURABILITY. A wall tile's body needn't be super-tough, so most are thinner than tiles intended for floors and counters. Many floor tiles, however, are rated for strength.

The simplest scale divides floor tiles into four use ratings: light duty, medium duty, heavy duty, and commercial. While medium- and even light-duty materials may be adequate for a bathroom floor, you'll probably want heavy-duty tiles for a kitchen or family room.

Some tiles are also rated for glaze hardness—their resistance to scuffing and abrasion. Common systems include the Abrasive Wear Index and the Mohs hardness test. Though you won't need a high rating for wall tiles, you certainly will for an entry floor or kitchen counter. Generally, an Index rating of 3 or a Mohs rating of 7 translates to heavy-duty tile.

SLIP RESISTANCE. Tiles destined for interior floors, stair treads, showers, and patios must provide adequate traction for safe walking, whether wet or dry. Generally speaking, unglazed, textured tiles offer better traction than glazed versions, though some glazed floor tiles include enough texture or abrasive additives for safe footing. Unglazed mosaics also work well, since their many grout lines help break up the surface.

Some manufacturers rate tiles with a so-called "coefficient of friction"; your dealer can interpret this for you and make recommendations.

STAIN RESISTANCE. Kitchen countertops, kitchen and bathroom floors, tub surrounds, fireplace faces, and patios are areas with high potential for staining. Dense tiles and those with sturdy glazes are best bets here. Sealers (see page 97) help protect porous tiles, but may be unsafe for use on eating and food-preparation surfaces.

FREEZE-THAW STABILITY. Tiles used outdoors in cold climates must be able to withstand water absorption and seasonal temperature fluctuations without warping or breaking. In these areas, impervious or vitreous tiles are usually the safest. This is less of an issue in mild climates, where softer, more absorbent tiles like terra-cotta can be acceptable choices.

WHAT IS TILE, ANYWAY?

Today's ceramic tiles consist of natural clays with additives such as talc or powdered shale to extend the clay and cut down on shrinkage. Most commercial tiles are formed by either the *dust-press method* or by *extrusion*. Dust-pressing entails injecting premixed, nearly dry ingredients into steel dies and subjecting them to enormous pressure. Extruded tiles are squeezed through a set of rollers (picture a giant pasta machine), then cut to size. Compared to precise, crisp dust-press tiles, extruded tiles are mildly irregular—though some manufacturers regrind them to make them more uniform.

In either case, the result—the *green* tile—is fired in a kiln, after which it becomes the *bisque.* Generally, the longer the firing and the hotter the temperature, the tougher and more water resistant the final product. For unglazed tiles, such as terra-cotta, this is the end of the line. But most tiles are then surfaced with one or more thin layers of *glaze* and refired.

Handmade art tiles are often formed in more labor-intensive ways and glazed and painted by hand. And some popular unglazed tiles, such as Mexican saltillos, are still laid out to bake in the sun in the time-honored way; prized tiles bear imprints where dog paws or chicken feet or even leaves have touched damp surfaces.

Most natural stone tiles are first split or gang-cut with diamond saws, then polished and cut into individual units. Not all are polished to a high luster. Increasingly popular are so-called "reverse-polishing" processes, including honing, resawing, and etching. These all furnish rougher, matte finishes—as does "tumbling," which gives an antique-like patina to marble tiles. Some stone tiles, notably slate, are simply split along existing seams, yielding hard, natural-looking, slightly irregular faces.

designing with tile

NOW YOU *can begin to fine-tune your decorating plans. As you'll see, tile is an effective medium for evoking both style and mood. The design effects you create result from your conscious manipulation of color, pattern, texture, size, and shape. Beginning on page 31, you'll find scores of room-specific ideas for tile installations. Here, we present some basic design concepts. Remember that these are reliable guidelines, not strict rules.*

Focus or backdrop?

If you're ready to enter the design process, first ask yourself whether tile should be the focus or the backdrop of your room. More specifically, should it call attention to itself and create its own flashy, charismatic drama, with other furnishings fairly neutral, or should it serve as a supporting background for other decorative elements in the space? Few interior designs, especially brightly colored or heavily patterned ones, can flourish with more than one main focus.

Given the spectrum of colors and array of shapes in which tile comes, it's relatively easy to use it to create visual drama. Part of the fun of today's tile renaissance is seeing the almost limitless stock of vibrant colors and patterns now available.

On the other hand, an understated tile backdrop can handsomely support more attention-getting furnishings, wall coverings, window treatments, and accessories. When deciding, remember that it's simpler to change furniture and fabrics than to redo a relatively permanent tile installation.

Tile style

A decorating style has physical characteristics that identify it with a particular region, era, or artistic movement—English Victorian, Southwestern, Arts and Crafts, Art Deco, and so on. Because certain tiles are linked to certain historic decorating styles, they can be used to evoke the character of a period—or simply to personalize and give dignity to a bland modern house.

Even so, rarely are styles slavish replicas of historical designs. More typically, designers select among elements that echo the mood of a period or regional look. A mood is the ambience that develops when a style is interpreted in a particular context—cozy, inviting, serene, or precise. What matters is that you choose a style and mood you find sympathetic and comfortable.

On the following three pages, we take a tour of five basic design styles, including period, regional, romantic, country, and contemporary. We also show a sampling of tile types that are linked with each look. Use this information as a starting point for your own explorations.

INTERIOR DESIGNER: JANNA LUND RODGERS

TILE ARTISANS: AHMED AGRAMA & TAMARA HARRIS

PERIOD STYLE

Old and reproduction homes often are decorated in a style that suits their architecture. Popular tile motifs include quaint Dutch figures (near left) and Arts and Crafts frogs (bottom left). Classic white-trimmed fireplace and hearth (far left) are faced with Dutch delftware.

REGIONAL STYLE

Responding to climate, indigenous resources, and cultural sensibilities, regional styles frequently include tile. Mexican saltillos and handpainted accents (near left) have a Mediterranean air; Malibu tile (bottom left) is symbolic of sunny Southern California in the early 1900s. The interlocking designs on fireplace and hearth (far left) are hallmarks of Moroccan tile style.

ROMANTIC STYLE

*Usually graceful and feminine, "romantic" isn't strictly a style but more
an intimate mood. Victorian decors are often romantic, but those of other
periods may be as well. Floral tiles in both French faience* (above left)
and Victorian transfer (above right) *versions fill the bill. The romantic
master bath* (right) *is dressed in soft colors and florals, including an
elegant handpainted ceramic sink.*

DESIGN: COUNTRY FLOORS

ARCHITECT: REMICK ASSOCIATES ARCHITECTS-BUILDERS, INC.

COUNTRY STYLE

*To some, country is rustic, distressed, or quaint; to others, it is Shaker-
simple, with minimal but distinctive accessories. It can be casual, formal,
or eclectic. In tile, country kitchens often employ naturalistic themes like
flowers, fruits* (both shown above), *and vegetables. The formal country
kitchen* (left) *is lavishly dressed with tile, including ornate relief trim and
handpainted murals on both vent hood and backsplash.*

CONTEMPORARY STYLE

Contemporary design tends to be sleek, strong, and graphic, with bold colors or shapes set against plain backgrounds. Machine-made ceramic or stone tiles can be highlighted with bright, playful accents (left). Or keep the look monolithic, as shown in the stone-lined kitchen (above).

Color

Because color packs such emotional punch, it's of primary importance when decorating. What colors are you most comfortable with? Your current furnishings, clothing, and accessories offer clues. Quickly browse through the gallery of examples in the following chapter, thinking only of color; make note of any strong likes or dislikes.

One familiar rule of color design is that light tones make surroundings seem larger, where as dark colors tend to shrink space.

Whites, creams, and neutrals are traditional favorites and always in style. White reflects and maximizes whatever light is available. A light, neutral background gives you the freedom to use color in furnishings to focus your design.

Warm colors, such as peach, yellow, and terra-cotta, appear to advance, making a room seem cozier. They're favorites for romantic and country design schemes. They can also help dimly lit or north-facing spaces seem less cool. Warm colors are flattering to skin tones, making them natural choices for powder rooms and entertaining spaces.

Blue, green, and violet, on the other hand, are cool, serene hues. Black adds drama but absorbs light and seems to shrink room size. High contrast has the same impact as a dark color: it adds impact but reduces the perceived space.

▪ **MONOCHROMATIC** color schemes, often white-on-white, set up a classic backdrop for furnishings and accents. Using subtle colors throughout a room can unify the space and make

A monochromatic, white-on-white scheme spreads light and wraps this master bath in quiet, classic style. Tile shapes and sizes are artfully varied for subtle visual interest; matching trim and border tiles help ease transitions.

awkward details less obvious. But the danger of a monochromatic scheme is that it can be boring. Use shapes, textures, and borders to produce subtle variations. Consider floating a few decorative tiles in a white or neutral field. Remember that all-white or all-dark schemes are the toughest to keep looking clean; texture (see page 24) helps camouflage dirt.

- **ANALOGOUS** color schemes (using closely related colors) may provide more variety than monochromatic plans. They typically employ three to five hues of one primary color.
- **COMPLEMENTARY** color schemes use hues directly opposite each other on the color wheel—for example, yellow and violet. Depending on the hues, the effect can be either startling or satisfying. This way of handling color usually works best if one of the colors is used more prominently than the other.

Don't forget, fixtures and appliances have color that you may need to consider. Some manufacturers make this process simpler by offering coordinated lines of wall, floor, and trim tiles; other lines match wallpapers, countertop surfaces, and even bathroom fixtures. If you just can't find the color you need, most dealers can special-order a custom color—for a price.

The quality of light greatly affects color. Direct sun, shade, and artificial incandescent, fluorescent, and halogen sources all can render tile hues differently. That's why it's important to examine a sample of the tile you think you want to use under different lighting conditions—preferably in the room where it will be installed.

DESIGN: ANN SACKS TILE & STONE

This shower design is a textbook example of complementary colors—specifically, the triad of orange, purple, and green. In this case, the hues are gentle and are tempered further by the creamy beige in both center tiles and grout spaces.

DESIGN: MINOR REVISIONS ARCHITECTURE & DESIGN. CONTRACTOR: MARK McCARTHY. TILE: AMAFI TILE & MARBLE

DESIGN: TAYLOR WOODROW

Two graphic patterns are shown here. Staggered, handmade field tiles (far left) are joined by smaller relief dots on a shower wall. The limestone floor (left) is jazzed up with bold stripes and accents made from granite and glass tiles.

Pattern

The modular nature of tile shapes and sizes provides almost unlimited pattern potential for those wishing to mix and match. High-contrast patterns like checkerboards have obvious drama, but subtler patterns can be created using mono-chromatic or analogous colors and mixed textures.

The obvious rule about patterns is that small ones are best for small spaces, large ones for large spaces. Complex patterns can feel confining and can disappear in a big room. Simple, open patterns tie together large spaces and lend a sense of freedom and calm.

Patterns can be naturalistic, stylized, geo-metrical, or abstract. Naturalistic renderings of natural forms, such as flowers, are popular in period, romantic, and country styles (see pages 17–19). On the other hand, geometric, random, and other nonrepresentational patterns fit with most contemporary designs.

Consider the lines formed by the tiles. A repeated floor pattern that runs lengthwise adds depth to a room; running across, it gives a shorter, wider look. Setting tile in a diagonal layout creates a more dynamic rhythm. A busy tile pattern or a mix of several colors makes an area look smaller; using a simple pattern or a single color has the opposite effect.

Airy, quiet patterns allow you to link large areas or a suite of several rooms. Trim and border tiles link patterns and also allow you to define distinct focal points and activity areas. For example, a tiled "area rug" beneath a dining table visually distinguishes this space from the surrounding room.

Don't forget that grout—the cement- or epoxy-base filler between tiles—affects your tile pattern. Unless you wish to play up the grid-like design, pick a grout color that blends with field tiles: light for light installations, dark for dark designs. For decorative tiles, aim to match the grout to the tiles' background color. The width of grout lines also has an effect. Narrow spaces seem to drop away; wider lines create a bolder sense of pattern. See page 29 for more help on choosing and using grout.

The tiles in this bathroom (facing page) are a near-riot of color but artfully laid out. Elements are formed with inexpen-sive, readily available wall tiles in 1- to 6-inch squares, plus trim and cut triangles.

The lion-headed wall fountain and spa (above) *contrast diagonal checkerboard diamonds in glossy colors with an earthier backdrop of larger backyard brick. Tough, easy-to-clean porcelain relief tiles* (facing page) *add texture to rangeside backsplash and vent hood.*

Texture

Less obvious than color and pattern, texture has a major effect on both. Highly polished tiles intensify colors and read as formal. A play of light reflected from glossy surfaces creates brightness, but brings with it a harder, cooler, more high-tech look. Matte finishes and unglazed terra-cotta create a warmer, more casual mood and make spaces feel more intimate. In general, textured tiles are also easier to blend with other elements in the room.

Texture in tile may be perceived either tactilely or visually. Your fingers can feel the sensation of changes in the plane from matte or pebbly glazes, relief patterns, or pockmarks on a tumbled-marble surface. Visual textures are like special effects: the surfaces look varied, but in fact are smooth to the touch.

When considering texture, think about maintenance. Glossy tiles are simple to keep clean but quickly show whatever dirt or grease is present.

Porous tiles with rough textures tend to stain, but mask it better. A good compromise may be a tile with visual texture—one that's smooth but has a shaded or flecked glaze.

Size and shape

When selecting a size, again the guideline is small tiles for small spaces, large tiles for large rooms. If the tile's scale is too large for a room, the effect will be overpowering. If it's too small, the design will look weak. Squares and rectangles are considered stable shapes; diamonds and triangles add movement.

Because it's difficult to align tiles on adjacent walls and floors, it's best to stagger tile shapes or to work with different sizes. Most installations are intentionally bottom-heavy; that is, they vary from smaller (walls) through medium (countertops) to large (floor) sizes. Another tactic is to organize the floor layout on the diagonal, or set it off from walls with a decorative border.

INTERIOR DESIGNER: MONA BRANAGH/PACIFIC BAY INTERIORS

gearing up

INSTALLING *ceramic tile can be a sizable financial commitment. Be sure to shop around, calculate costs, and order carefully. Remember, it's best to select the tile that's most suitable for the projected use, then consider appearance. Your tile dealer can help with fine points, once you've done the basic research. If you're planning a large installation or are simply overwhelmed by the choices, an architect, designer, or tile contractor can help you winnow down and establish priorities.*

Showroom savvy

A well-stocked tile center has as many luscious colors and alluring shapes as an old-fashioned candy store; just looking brings on an appetite. But remind yourself, looks aren't enough. The tile you choose must be right for your needs. DO YOUR HOMEWORK. Browse through books (like this one), magazines, advertisements, and brochures. Compile a scrapbook of possibilities that appeal to you. You may wish to take a cue from interior designers and create a sample board showing wallpaper and fabric swatches, paint chips, and fixture colors. Also, take rough measurements of your room.

Most tile professionals are knowledgeable and ready to help. They can answer your questions and advise you on tile aesthetics, tile quality, the number of tiles you'll require, and the costs involved in your project. If you've fallen in love with a beautiful but impractical

DESIGN: COUNTRY FLOORS

tile, a good dealer can help you find something similar that holds up better.

Must the tile be waterproof, slip resistant, scuff resistant, easy to maintain, or stable outdoors in freezing weather? Your dealer can verify these properties or refer you to manufacturers' specifications. Be sure the maker's warranty covers the uses you've planned.

Often you can borrow samples to try at home for color, size, and compatibility. Buy a sample of the tile, if necessary. If you own it, you can also test it for scuffing (rub a metal cooking pot against it), smudging, and ease of cleanup.

Most retailers have displays or catalogs of tiles they don't carry in stock. You may have to wait a long time for certain styles, so get reliable information on availability and plan accordingly. **MONEY-SAVING TIPS.** The costs of ceramic tile run from modest to very expensive—from a bargain-basement $1 per square foot for remainders up to $50 and more for one-of-a-kind art tiles, and even more for some stones.

Single-color glazed wall tiles—those commonly used around showers and tubs—are the most economical. The trim pieces for these tiles normally cost more per square foot than do the field tiles. The addition of three-dimensional patterns and multicolored glazes can easily double costs.

If you're on a tight budget, remember these hints:

- **WATCH FOR CLOSEOUTS** that a dealer will sell at a discount. These may be lines that manufacturers have discontinued, colors or patterns that were overstocked, or tiles left over from a large job or cancelled order.
- **SHOP FOR SECONDS;** these tiles are flawed or blemished (usually only slightly), so they cannot be sold with the regular stock at full price. Often, seconds will go undetected if randomly mixed with unblemished tiles.
- **RESERVE COSTLIER ART TILES** as accents in a simpler field of stock wall tile. Space them at regular intervals or sprinkle them randomly. Not only will this kind of plan stretch your budget, it will also help showcase those one-of-a-kind tiles you've fallen in love with.

A colorful wall's worth of European mural tiles (facing page) *is sure to get your creative juices flowing. A stone showroom's sample display* (below) *graphically shows part of the amazing range available.*

Making the purchase

Once you're in the final stages, have accurate measurements drawn up for the area to be covered. A plan on graph paper helps you visualize the area and provides clues to the trim pieces you may need. Or use a computer drawing program and a color printer to try out more involved patterns on paper.

When figuring your needs, remember that actual tile sizes may vary from the nominal sizes listed. For example, if your selection is a 6 by 6 glazed wall tile, it may actually be $3/8$ inch smaller or larger. Either measure the tile yourself or verify its dimensions with your dealer.

With your drawing in hand, a tile dealer should be able to help you figure out how many tiles you'll require. Be sure to buy extra tiles—the rule of thumb is 5 percent, though tricky installations may require an extra 10 percent. This allows for breakage during cutting. And if a tile chips after installation, you'll have a replacement on hand—whereas if you wait until damage occurs to search for new tiles, you may not be able to find pieces that match.

Skilled tile artisans produce many one-of-a-kind designs, like this exuberantly swirled shower mosaic.

TILE ARTISAN: MARLO BARTELS STUDIO OF LAGUNA BEACH

Before you bring the tiles home, check the cartons to be sure the colors match. Different cartons of the same tile can vary significantly. Check that "shade lot" numbers are the same from box to box. Even so, most installers mix these boxes together before beginning the job.

Need help?

For a price, you won't need to go it alone when either choosing or installing your new tile. Design help is available from architects, interior designers and decorators, and kitchen and bath professionals. Tile contractors handle the installation process.

Architects specialize in suiting form to function. They can help you analyze your particular needs and find solutions to tricky remodeling problems. Of course, some architects may be more concerned with structural solutions than aesthetics.

Interior designers and decorators may be more attuned to tile style, scale, pattern, and color. Kitchen and bath designers may also know the latest on tile styles and installation glitches. All of these professionals can gain you access to trade-only showrooms and services you might not be able to find for yourself.

Tile contractors can show you samples and advise you on some basic choices, but it's best to already have preferences in mind from your own legwork. The contractor can also advise you on potential structural problems, such as whether your subfloor will support a heavy tile floor without requiring either bolstering or waterproofing.

While today's modern adhesives and grouts have made some tile-setting jobs a snap, the experienced hand of a licensed contractor is still crucial for many projects. For example, installing swimming pool tile is not do-it-yourself work. Applications that require setting tiles in a full mortar bed, such as around a free-form or sunken tub, are best handled by a professional. And a contractor can take on an awkward space that requires a lot of matching of surfaces and/or intricate cuts.

TILE SETTING: HOW THE PROS DO IT

Should you try tiling it yourself? If you're handy, and if your project is a simple backsplash, countertop, or rectangular floor, you might venture the work yourself. The overview given here provides a basic gloss of the tiling process.

A quality tile installation is an integrated "sandwich," including not just tile but also an appropriate backing material, a setting bed of thin-set mortar or adhesive, and grout to seal and decorate the edges.

You can install new tile over new or existing gypsum wallboard, cement backerboard, exterior-grade plywood, or even wood paneling or existing tile as long as it's in good condition. Don't try to install tile over a springy surface; any movement will cause the grout and tile to crack. If there is a great deal of bounce in a floor, you may need to have a professional install a so-called "floating floor" first.

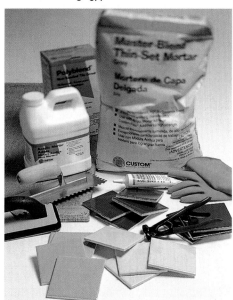

In areas that have to withstand a lot of moisture, such as a shower or tub enclosure, the best choice of backing is cement backerboard, which will not disintegrate when wet. To keep water out of the wall, put a moisture barrier over the backing. Waterproof membrane comes in three basic forms: tar paper, CPE sheets, and a kit consisting of reinforcing fabric and liquid rubber.

Ceramic tile may be set in either a thick bed of mortar or a thinner combed-out bed of mortar or adhesive. Though setting tile in thick traditional mortar gives best results for bathroom tub and shower enclosures, this work is definitely a job for a professional. You can choose from three types of thin-set adhesive—cement-base, organic-base, or epoxy-base. Cement-base thin-set mortars are the pro's choice in most cases, though organic adhesives or *mastics* are suitable in spots that won't see much traffic or be exposed to much moisture. Epoxy products are super-tough but more expensive.

Though grout may seem like a minor player, the time to consider it is early on in your planning. Cement-base grout is the traditional choice, and is adequate for many applications. In bathrooms and kitchens, a mildew-resistant version is in order. Applying a grout sealer can help cement-base grout stand up to both moisture and stains.

Epoxy grouts, while more expensive, are better than cement-base for wet areas and spots where food and chemical stains collect. In most cases you won't need to seal an epoxy grout.

As detailed on page 23, grout color can have a major impact on the overall color and pattern of a tile installation. Grouts now come in a wide selection of colors, in both sanded and non-sanded versions. Choose a non-sanded grout for glazed wall tiles and other machine-made units where grout spacings are 1/8 inch or less. Larger spacings—for example, those between irregular handmade or terra-cotta tiles—call for the extra body and strength of sanded grout.

Where horizontally laid tile meets a perpendicular surface of tile or or another material, use caulking compound—not grout—to fill the joint. This allows the surfaces to flex slightly, minimizing stress cracks in both tile and grout. You'll find that caulking compounds now come in most of the same colors that grout does.

RESIDENTIAL DESIGNER: ROB MORRIS

GREAT TILE IDEAS

IN THE FIRST chapter, "A Planning Primer,"
we explored the principles of choosing tile and creating decorative effects with it. Now we're going
for inspiration—this time room by room. **SUBSECTIONS** of this chapter present an exciting
array of tile installations, in four zones of the home: kitchen, bathroom, living space, and outdoors.
You'll discover a rainbow of colorful ideas for each of these areas, plus space-specific planning
pointers. Do you lean toward a traditional sense of repose, a casual country ambience, or a bolder,
more modern blast of color? Whatever your taste, you should find sympathetic examples here, as
we've aimed to present as broad a spectrum of styles as possible. For specific design guidelines, see
pages 16–25. **BROWSE AT YOUR** leisure, perhaps marking your favorite pictures to show a
tile supplier or designer. Many of these ideas can be adapted from one room for another, and they
can be scaled up or down depending on your needs. For background on the tile types shown here,
see "A Shopper's Guide," beginning on page 91.

kitchens

IN LIGHT of the kitchen's central role in household activities, its surfaces must stand up to repeated scrapes and scuffs, spills, steamy pasta pots, and messy school projects. Sturdy, watertight, easy-to-clean tile is the natural choice here, especially since the options are so plentiful.

The two main poles of kitchen style are *country* and *contemporary*. With the right tile (see pages 17–19), you can easily accomplish either look, as well as a full spectrum of period and regional themes. Country kitchens, with earth-tone floors in quarry tile or terra-cotta, often use the backsplash space for tiles with cheerful fruit or floral motifs or for informal decorative murals or for a display of homey handmade or art tiles. High-tech contemporary kitchens are streamlined for efficiency; their sleek, no-nonsense air is often best served by machine-made glazed tiles, typically in white or neutrals, that form a background for gleaming pans, clean-lined cabinets, and perhaps a few accents such as well-placed art tiles. There are always exceptions to these generalities. Some of the most dramatic kitchen designs borrow playfully and shamelessly from the whole range of traditions.

Backsplash basics. The backsplash—the wall area between countertop and wall cabinets—is a premier destination for decorative tile, be it a few colorful art tiles in a quiet field, a classic floral mural, or a jazzier art mosaic. This blank "canvas" is typically about 18 inches tall and set about 36 to 54 inches off

Lively-looking contemporary backsplash features variegated relief art tiles in Paul Klee colors.

DESIGN: LOU ANN BAUER

the floor. You can match countertop tile (see below), contrast it, echo the countertop's trim, or flaunt another look entirely. Use trim where the backsplash meets countertop tile, or simply run the tile down to another counter material and caulk the joint (see page 29).

Counter intelligence. There are pros and cons to tiling countertops. On the positive side, tile is attractive and watertight; on the minus side, it can seem cold, uneven, and hard to clean. If you choose another countertop material, such as stone, wood, laminate, or solid-surface, you can still feature tile on the backsplash—and perhaps use a heatproof tiled counter insert near the cooktop or work area.

If you decide to tile the countertops, machine-made tiles work best because of their greater uniformity. The tiles you choose should be highly stain resistant and, if glazed, resistant to acids and household chemicals. Be sure to ask your dealer if the tiles you like are rated for countertops. Think twice about dark, glossy glazes—they show every stain and smudge. And be careful about sealers: many are inappropriate for eating and food-preparation surfaces.

For a smoother surface that's easier to clean, consider using large uniform floor tiles with narrow grout lines. Choose a mildew-resistant grout.

Of course, you may also decide to tile a kitchen island, eating peninsula, or breakfast table, too.

Hardworking floors. Kitchen floors take a pounding. So in most cases, you'll be looking for tough tiles that can stand up to water, spills, and dropped pots while remaining slip resistant and good-looking to boot. Impossible? Porcelain pavers, quarry tiles, glazed floor tiles, and some stones can fill the bill, and you'll find enough color options in all these to build whatever pattern you choose. Terra-cotta creates an appealingly rustic ambience, but should be sealed.

Diamond-shaped limestone accents march across a kitchen floor of sealed saltillo pavers.

DESIGN: GEOFFREY FROST/KITCHEN STUDIO LOS ANGELES

For a floating, seamless look, consider tiling the spaces below cabinets—called *kickspaces* or *toe spaces*—to match floor or backsplash. If tiling is all you're doing, it's simplest to lay new tiles up to existing cabinet lines (though this can limit later access to pullout appliances). With a major remodel, it's usually best to tile the whole space before adding cabinets and appliances. While you're at it, it's a good time to install a cozy, nonallergenic radiant-heat system below the new floor.

The stove area. Think about two other prominent focal points: the vent hood and the range surround. Tiled vent hoods are traditional in country designs, and clearly symbolize the warmth of "hearth and home." Colorful Portuguese, Spanish, or Mexican tiles are popular here; they often sport culinary or floral motifs as well as more stylized patterns. This space is also a good place to display pictorial compositions, such as a tiled fruit bowl, wildflower bouquet, or pastoral mural. Contemporary vent hoods might feature a single trim row of colorful wall or art tiles that repeat backsplash or floor motifs.

The alcove that houses a freestanding range, be it a vintage model or a modern residential/commercial behemoth, is another good location for decorative tile. Even in a streamlined built-in design, you'll still often see a special tiled motif behind the cooktop.

Formal as can be, this floor features 24-by 24-inch polished-marble squares framed by bands of smaller limestone tiles. Countertops are surfaced with solid limestone in the same creamy beige.

Bright glazed tile in a rich pumpkin adds a punch of color to this efficient, sophisticated kitchen designed with fuss-free materials for minimal maintenance.

Details, details. Wainscoting (a half-wall of tile) or a simple chair rail (a single or double row at "chair height") can help define a breakfast area or office alcove, perhaps echoing a motif in backsplash, vent hood, or floor. Window and door trim can also be tiled to match.

Details can custom-finish the look. You might create tiled wall niches for spices, oils, and utensils. Open shelves and open alcoves for pots and pans look more integrated when tiled. Tiled decks inside greenhouse windows appear more finished and help ward off moisture damage.

DESIGN: TAYLOR WOODROW

DESIGN: BRAD POLVOROSA

A rich and playful back-splash mosaic of smashed green tile shards sets off the cherry cabinets, commercial range, and brushed-steel vent hood. Glass accent spheres are scattered throughout the tile, sparkling like colored jewels.

*French terra-cotta pavers
add a traditional touch to
a thoroughly modern kitchen
that also features a celadon-
and-white tiled island
and granite-topped work
surfaces. Radiant heating
below the pavers keeps the
floor warm, as enjoyed
by the cat.*

DESIGN: BENEDIKT STREBEL CERAMICS

What if a different orientation were rendered atop the regular grid of a floor tile? You'd get a dynamic, multidirectional design like this one, handpainted in sharp angles, squiggles, swirls, and craggy textures like abstract art.

Field tiles and borders with variegated pastel glazes line an under-sink niche recessed in a country kitchen's pickled-pine cabinetry. Patterned encaustic tiles form the floor.

The backsplash for this small serving counter and throughout the kitchen combines slate tile in two natural colors—green and dark gray.

DESIGN: COUNTRY FLOORS

TILES: MARGARET VALENTINE

Custom oversize tiles serve two functions in this English Country kitchen: they reinforce the decorating theme and also provide a fireproof backsplash for the range alcove. Dimensional fleurs-de-lis and sunburst shapes, fired with the glazed yellow tiles, add decorative accents.

Tough, earth-toned quarry tiles line the hard-working countertops of this Southwest-style kitchen; they're joined by colorful, handmade art tiles in backsplash areas.

TILE ARTISAN: KAREN KOBLITZ

DESIGN: MINOR REVISIONS ARCHITECTURE & DESIGN.
CONTRACTOR: MARK McCARTHY. TILE: BUDDY RHODES STUDIO/AMALFI TILE & MARBLE.

*Exuding a quiet
respect for tradition,
this design incorporates
both translucent glazed
field tiles and cast
ceramic pieces. Gleaming
carved ceramic columns
seem to hold the vent
hood aloft; for contrast,
glaze was removed
from the backsplash's
centerpiece wreath.*

*A kitchen island's sturdy
countertop, surfaced with
1- by 1-inch Venetian glass
mosaics, sits a level above
a marble-look floor of
concrete field tiles and
smaller concrete accents.*

DESIGN: BRAD POLVOROSA

TILE ARTISAN: RODGER DUNHAM CERAMIC DESIGN OF PETALUMA

Honoring the Victorian heritage of the house, the kitchen remodel incorporated antique plates set into diagonally laid field tiles. The plates were "floated" in a thick layer of mortar; then tiles were painstakingly hand-cut to fit around them.

Cows amble across a pastoral vista and stare placidly out at the owners of this handpainted back-splash mural. Large tiles with thin grout lines keep the composition unified.

DESIGN: TAYLOR WOODROW

Granite tiles sheathe island and countertops in this kitchen. In the cooktop alcove, granite gives way to a diagonally laid slate backsplash panel with glass-mosaic borders and accents.

Mustard-color 6- by 6-inch tiles on countertops and walls with hand-painted Mexican borders and diamond-shaped relief accents brighten this Mediterranean-inspired design. Dark-stained wood edgings and cabinets make a rich contrast.

Why not tile a table's top? This one has black-and-white checkerboard wall tiles around a painted faux-marble center.

great tile ideas

bathrooms

THOROUGHLY time-tested since the days of ancient baths, tile is a tried-and-true performer in modern bathrooms as well. Properly installed, it's highly water resistant, easy to clean, and hygienic.

The design possibilities are endless—from elegant repose to romantic Victorian florals, from monochromatic neutrals to riotous color patterns. Both stone and handmade wall tiles add texture, as do the many options in relief borders (often with appropriate marine themes). New terrazzo, glass, and concrete tiles are showing up here, too. Custom art mosaics, handmade art tiles, and murals abound.

But even plain, inexpensive tiles can be combined to bold effect. Just mixing and matching among the many available colors and sizes of commercial wall tile provides almost inexhaustible options.

Design strategies depend in part on how the bathroom is used. Is it a master bath, guest bath, or kids' bath? The master bath, increasingly treated as part of a larger master-suite layout, is private, and design possibilities are wide open. Choose any tile that's stylish and practical and that fits your budget.

Guest baths and powder rooms are at least partially for company. These less-used spaces can be places to enjoy working with less heavy-duty materials. These spaces tend to be smaller than master baths, so a little splurge can go a long way.

Children's baths are in particular need of tile's toughness and water-

Stone-textured concrete tiles are wrapped in square-within-square fashion by contrasting concrete rectangles and small square accents. The glass baseboard shows just how well mosaics can handle curves.

DESIGN: MINOR REVISIONS ARCHITECTURE & DESIGN. CONTRACTOR: MARK McCARTHY. TILE: BUDDY RHODES STUDIO/AMALFI TILE & MARBLE

DESIGN: MINOR REVISIONS ARCHITECTURE & DESIGN. CONTRACTOR: MARK McCARTHY. TILE: AMALFI TILE & MARBLE

shedding abilities. Have fun, but remember that tile lasts a long time. The cowboy theme that suited your six-year-old might be viewed with great disdain in later years.

Waterworks. Built-in tubs are usually framed by three walls that are tiled to the ceiling or to door or window height. If there's no shower head, you could stop the tile at a lower level. A tiled pedestal or platform helps link the tub to the rest of the room. Tubside tile should ideally be watertight, though with a good backing (see page 29) you can also consider the many glazed wall tiles available. Art tiles, decorative borders, and murals help enliven this area.

Built-in showers are ideal for tiling, too, both inside and out. Frame the opening with borders or handmade art tiles; a clear glass door lets you see the tile display inside, too. Unglazed mosaics make a tough, skid-resistant shower floor. You'll probably want to tile the shower ceiling as well— perhaps diagonally, so it won't fight with wall patterns.

For ease of maintenance, consider gloss or matte-textured wall tiles that are tightly butted with minimal grout lines. Plan to install them with non-staining, mildew-resistant grout. Remember that dark-colored, high-gloss tiles can be difficult to keep looking clean.

Floor options. Bathroom floors should deliver style, protection against moisture and stains, and secure footing. Porcelain pavers, glazed floor tiles, and mosaics work best, but terra-cotta and other soft tiles can be adequate if sealed. Slate, limestone, and marble are popular choices for elegant master baths and powder rooms. It's best to choose matte textures for slip-resistance, or add mats or nonslip rugs as needed. A light-use powder room could be floored with wall tiles. To keep the floor design from fighting wall patterns, choose a different tile size or lay tiles on the diagonal.

A classic monochromatic scheme blends limestone-like field tiles with a border of handmade relief tiles.

Installing a radiant heat system under the floor makes a tiled floor more comfortable on cold mornings.

On the countertop. Bathroom countertops and backsplashes are two more surfaces waiting to be tiled. Some wall tiles are adequate here (ask your dealer's advice), but be sure their glaze is tough enough to stand up to scratches, household cleaners, and cosmetic potions like nail polish remover. Ceramic and stone floor tiles are generally tougher, and their larger expanses mean fewer grout joints.

Backsplashes are also a good place to add subtle or not-so-subtle art tiles and mosaics. Mirrors are frequently trimmed in tile. Look for color-coordinated electric outlet and switch plates. With a pedestal sink, consider running a tile backsplash to the floor both for water protection and a flash of style. Pedestal sinks eliminate the bulk of a vanity, but also do away with the cabinet's storage space. To compensate, you might want to have a tiled storage niche between wall studs or a tiled ledge behind the sink to house toothbrushes, soap, and water glasses.

Eye-catching details. Accessories are the icing on the cake. Examine what's available in ceramic soap dishes, towel bars and hooks, and cup holders. A handpainted ceramic sink might beautifully tie things together. Remember that some commercial tiles are color-matched to lines of ceramic sinks, tubs, toilets, and bidets.

Bathrooms are tempting backdrops for intricate tile wainscoting, chair rails, and subtler wall patterns inspired by the explosion of new trim and border tiles. But it's sometimes tricky to blend all these tiled surfaces, angles, and corners smoothly. For best results, test-drive your ideas ahead of time on paper or with the aid of a computer. Most dealers can help you work out the details.

A shower lined with serene, tropical blue-green glazed tiles is set off by a crisp all-white scheme in this appealing bathroom.

A luxurious master bath's carved wood-work is enhanced by dark green marble in 12- by 12-inch floor tiles and solid countertops.

ARCHITECT: MARY COLLINS/J. ALLEN SAYLES ARCHITECTS

ARCHITECT/BUILDER: LEON GOLDENBERG, MILFORD CUSTOM HOMES

DESIGN: TAYLOR WOODROW

Glass tiles in blue
and iridescent black trim
granite stripes on floor,
backsplash, and shower
(visible in the reflection).
Floors and countertops
are limestone tiles.

A master bathroom's open
shower/bath sports an
eclectic art mosaic and is
framed by extruded tiles
that closely mimic bamboo.
The random-laid floor
makes a neutral backdrop,
except for the colored
mosaic bits.

This classic Greek-key motif
laid out in 1-inch-square
tiles forms the border for
the floor and an accent
panel above the tub.

TILE ARTISAN: MARLO BARTELS STUDIO OF LAGUNA BEACH

ARCHITECT: REMICK ASSOCIATES ARCHITECTS-BUILDERS, INC.

ARCHITECT: KARDINAL ARCHITECTURAL SERVICES. TILE: BUDDY RHODES STUDIO

*A nondescript family
bath was given new
life with red-and-white
floor mosaics, a white-
tiled countertop, and
red liner accents that
set off the cabinets'
painted geometrics.*

*Large rectangular tiles
of custom concrete resemble
limestone but are easier
to care for. They line the
tub pedestal and walls,
matching the round tub's
cast-concrete deck.*

*Tiled "area rugs"
mark use areas and
lead the eye through a
narrow corridor bath
between two bedrooms.
Each rug's diagonals
and accents are set
within a field of larger
cream squares.*

DESIGN: GEOFFREY FROST/KITCHEN STUDIO LOS ANGELES. TILE ARTISAN: RICHARD KEIT

DESIGN: MALIBU CERAMIC WORKS

Here's some color for a morning wake-up! Vibrant red and turquoise Malibu tiles form an "area rug" in front of the sink; they're repeated in the backsplash above. The vanity front is painted to match.

Existing tiles elsewhere in the house were the inspiration for this powder-room remodel. New Spanish relief reproductions were mixed into the countertop (note the tricky sink cuts), a single-row backsplash, and the mirror's frame.

This master bath, designed to coexist with existing bath-rooms from the 1920s, is a striking example of balanced tile design. Floor diagonals of earthy quarry tile are echoed by diagonals on the countertops and backsplash; green trim tile fronts the cabinets. Matching Malibu designs are used on floor borders and backsplash, and the tub surround is marked by a complementary pattern.

ARCHITECT: REMICK ASSOCIATES ARCHITECTS-BUILDERS, INC. TILE: STONELIGHT TILE COMPANY

*Ancient mosaic techniques
are revived in a modern
bathroom and tub platform.
The inspiration was tile
found in one of the oldest
Christian buildings in the
Adriatic town of Aquileia.*

This shower (above, left) *offers a study in patterns: the intricate dividing rail separates the field above, with accents in a diamond configuration, from the square-and-dot pattern below.*

A checkerboard marble floor (matching the wainscoting) is studded with clear diamond accents emitting fiber-optic light from below—a nice touch in a guest powder room where users may be unfamiliar with the layout.

A new shower surround was the canvas for tumbled-marble rectangles laid as a herringbone-patterned field. Staggered spots are one-of-a-kind handmade art tiles. Color-matched grout becomes an active background element.

*Translucent glass relief
tiles with lively geometrics
are sprinkled along a single
row of white field tiles
to highlight a tile-topped
tub surround.*

A tiled chair rail in a make-up area divides traditional wallpaper above from painted plaster below. The rail includes twin cast-relief borders that bound a single row of limestone tiles with glass-mosaic accents.

DESIGN: TAYLOR WOODROW

A tub surround is wrapped in monochromatic splendor, meshing white diagonals, sink cap, diamond trim accents, and relief border. Tan-colored grout relates the tub to the floor tile.

DESIGN: KITCHENS & MORE

The space behind a pedestal sink can be awkward. Why not tile it for a bit of flash and extra splash protection? Here, the contrasting grid of dark grout between handmade tiles is definitely part of the pattern.

A tropical fish *(below)* peers *imperturbably from the oceanic backdrop of this bathroom wall. This custom work artfully blends both mural and mosaic techniques, as painted pieces follow natural contours instead of a rigid grid.*

This tub pedestal is clad in variegated handmade tiles adorned with traditional Arts and Crafts thistle-design squares. The field tiles run right up to the windowsill, enhancing the built-in feel.

TILE ARTISAN: MATHERS ROWLEY/FIREDRAKE STUDIOS

great tile ideas

living spaces

T**HOUGH WE'RE** all familiar with the use of tile in the kitchen and bathroom, why leave it at that? In Europe, the use of tile throughout the home is traditional, and with good reason: tile is durable, is cool in summer, and provides unlimited decorative opportunities.

Places to ponder include the entry, living room, dining room, and bedroom. Great-room layouts can especially benefit from tile's ability both to tie spaces together and to gracefully distinguish them.

Elegant entries. Both ceramic and stone offer abundant style options for entries, whether the style is formal or eclectic. The entry is a public space, offering a first glimpse of the ambience within. Why not greet guests with time-echoing marble, rugged but handsome slate, or pale limestone? Hard-wearing porcelain pavers or colorful glazed tile? Or earthy terra-cotta with spot accents, for a welcoming sense of easygoing individuality?

A flush-mounted fireplace and wood niche are lined with formal white-and-blue tiles.

Because it's subject to heavy foot traffic, tracked mud, and moisture, tile for entryways should be hard-working and resistant to both slipping and stains. Unglazed terra-cotta and porous stones should be sealed. Both for safety and for ease of maintenance, it's best to choose uniform tiles and set them closely together with minimal grout spaces.

Living-room options. Living-room tiles also range from formal to funky. Again, stone choices, such as marble, slate, and limestone, lend a formal air; terra-cotta signals "country comfort." There are many new

INTERIOR DESIGNER: THOMAS BARTLETT INTERIORS

options in both porcelain pavers and glazed floor tiles that convey a variety of design styles. Patterns can be quiet and serene or boldly geometric, or they can flow with subtle variations from room to room to link a great-room layout. Tiled "area rugs" help subdivide a large space, and borders similarly confine the eye.

The fireplace is a traditional destination for decorative tile, be it traditional Dutch or English, handmade Arts and Crafts, or an eclectic modern mosaic. If the tile is sufficiently high-fired, it's easily cleaned, impervious to heat, and can even wrap inside the firebox. Build up the mantel or hearth, or embed decorative tiles flush in surrounding plasterwork. Woodstove surrounds are also good settings for tile. But since fireplaces and stoves are finicky beasts, it's best to check local codes for requirements in your area.

Interior stairs often sport tile, too. Risers, the vertical parts, offer almost unlimited options. Sprinkle varying colors or patterns from riser to riser, if you like, or mix random art tiles with bold patterns, glazes, or relief designs. Treads, the parts you step on, are another matter: uniform nonslip tiles with bullnosed fronts or even wood edgings are advised for these areas.

Sunrooms and sitting rooms can benefit from tiled floors or walls that conserve heat in winter and slow temperature swings in summer. The darker and denser the tile, the better: terra-cotta, quarry tile, and stone—all at least $1/2$ inch thick—are good bets.

Fine dining. Don't forget stylish, easy-to-clean tile for the dining room. Rules for living-room floors apply here, though the dining room probably won't see as much use, and thus its tiles needn't be quite as tough. Subtle changes in shape, scale, or pattern can help define this space as part of a multiroom flow of field tiles. Within a defined dining area, tiled wainscoting or chair rails are two traditional ways to help distinguish subboundaries.

This colorful entry joins blue granite stair treads with intricate Moroccan tiles in floor and risers.

Bedside aesthetics. What about bedrooms? In today's master-suite layouts, tile can serve as integrated flooring and also as a major decorative element linking the traditional bedroom area with bathroom, dressing area, spa, exercise room, and/or office You can tile floors, headboards, nightstands, study areas, and makeup centers. Installing radiant heating under a new tile floor can provide warmth underfoot in chilly weather.

All the trimmings. Flat planes in living areas—walls and even ceilings—provide ready settings for many other tile effects. Base (floor) and crown (ceiling) moldings come in both ceramic and stone versions in a variety of profiles; you can also choose from myriad trim and border pieces (see pages 104–105).

Window jambs and sills, door casings, built-in window seats, and bay-window aprons can all be tiled. Why not add a decorative tiled arch above a bland tract home's interior passageway?

Tiled wainscoting lends a classic flourish to living rooms, and, especially, dining rooms. Or use a simple row or two of tile at chair-rail height, tied to a pattern in the floor or window trim. Repeat the pattern inside display niches or along built-in shelves. Feature prized antique or art tiles as collectibles, perhaps on a picture rail placed out of harm's way.

In the entry hall, a colorful mural or a tiled mirror might make a fresh and attractive greeting for guests.

Furnishings with flash. There's an upswing in the number of tiled accoutrements—coffee tables, end tables, buffets, and so on—that are making their way into living spaces. Why not commission a table from a tile artisan, build one from scratch, or dress up a junkyard find with whimsical hand-set mosaics?

Echo this theme subtly in an adjacent living area or dining room to help direct visitors' eyes to your home's interior.

An entry foyer combines large honed-marble squares with smaller, tumbled accent grids laid in a gentle arc to direct guests inside.

A tile artisan has tiled both easy chair and coffee table with exuberant art mosaics. Unlike most mosaics, these pieces skillfully blend both smooth arcs and disks with random broken pieces.

TILE ARTISAN: MARLO BARTELS STUDIO OF LAGUNA BEACH

DESIGN: PAT KULETO

INTERIOR DESIGNER: OSBURN DESIGN

*A free-form mosaic
wraps around the jambs
of an interior door;
it's made from factory-
assembled stone chips
premounted to larger
backing strips, then fitted
and grouted in place.
The mosaic mirrors add
a flourish.*

*Classical in feeling,
this living room is floored
completely in stone, with
pale travertine rectangles
in the foreground, red
travertine steps, and
antique Balinese pavers
in the space beyond.*

great tile ideas

INTERIOR DESIGNER: BAUER INTERIOR DESIGN. TILE: ELLE TERRY LEONARD/ARCHITECTURAL CERAMICS

*This Moorish-looking
ceramic fireplace is
a dramatic living-room
focal point. Cast,
handcarved sections and
many individual tiles
were hard-fired, then
carefully fitted on-site.
Warm light inside the
open grillwork reflects
off a copper lining.*

*A sitting-room fireplace
just off the kitchen is
dramatically framed by
colorful, custom relief
tiles and quieter, speckled
hearth tiles.*

ARCHITECT: ROBERT WYLIE

*The fireplace is a highly
visible showplace for
period styles and period
tiles—in this case, a
beautiful rendition of
Arts and Crafts repose.*

A tiled insert enlivens
the hardwood floor of
this Mission-style design.
To avoid cracks, it's best
to caulk, not grout, any
joints where tile meets
another material.

DESIGN: AMOROSO/HOLMAN DESIGN GROUP

DESIGN: TAYLOR WOODROW

The shapes and colors
of tumbled-marble floor
tiles and glass accents are
reproduced in paint on
the adjacent wall.

An "area rug" is precisely
formed in this tiled floor mural,
which blends motifs from both
Oriental rugs and Malibu tiles.

great tile ideas

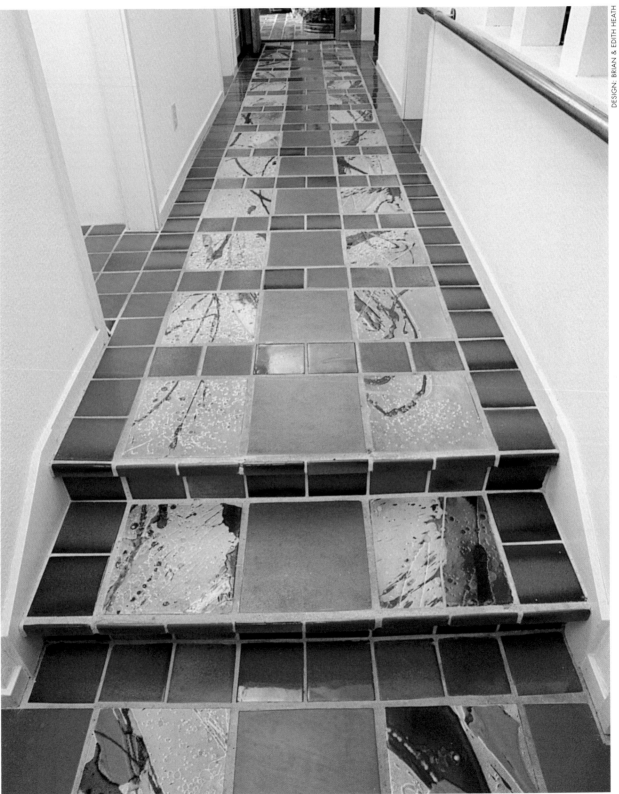

*A striking tile runner,
set in quiltlike fashion,
fills the interior hallway
and foreground stairs.*

DESIGN: BRIAN & EDITH HEATH

Stair risers make a highly visible accent and, because they're not actually walked upon, can feature glazed or relief tiles unsuitable for treads. These handpainted risers link foreground and staircase areas, with treads and flooring of classic Mediterranean terra-cotta.

Like a fanned-out deck of cards, this circular staircase is painstakingly dressed in a warm, earthy mosaic of old Mexican tiles. Myriad grout joints help furnish slip-resistant footing.

DESIGN: TAYLOR WOODROW

*Honed, sealed travertine
squares floor a master-suite
remodel, giving way in
the bedroom area to a
large gridwork of cast,
tinted concrete with
tiled travertine frames.
Channels were cut
for the tile strips after the
concrete was poured.*

*Tile can link the wide
spaces of a great-room
design, but sometimes
a uniform treatment gets
boring. In this case, the
pattern alters subtly and
the dominant stone colors
trade places as dining
room turns to kitchen.*

*A polished-marble and
limestone pattern flows
through the entry foyer
and across the front porch
and walk; the exterior
version has a less-slippery
honed finish.*

DESIGN: MINOR REVISIONS ARCHITECTURE & DESIGN. CONTRACTOR: MARK McCARTHY. TILE: BUDDY RHODES STUDIO/AMALFI TILE & MARBLE

*This dining room's
18-inch concrete tiles and
smaller 4-inch accents
have a marbleized finish.
The pattern repeats in the
adjacent open kitchen.*

great tile ideas

outdoor areas

TILED PATIOS are already common amenities in mild-weather regions. But the use of ceramic, stone, glass, and other tiles is quickly spreading to other exterior areas as we continue to enjoy extending our living spaces outdoors. Often-overlooked opportunities for tile include outdoor kitchens, barbecues, entertainment areas, and planting beds. Tile cladding also brings walls and exterior trim to colorful new life. And tile is perfect with water features: picture a pool dressed in playful art mosaics or in modern glass tiles that shimmer iridescently in the sunlight.

You may find that just a little outdoor tile is a great way to add style and to personalize a tract landscape, at the same time "stretching" the feel of your home's interior space. It's even better if the tile can be viewed from inside, too.

In contrast to the predictable path of concrete or brick, this path sports custom-painted, randomly placed striped tile squares.

Outdoor floors. First think of the backyard as an outdoor room, an extension of interior space. Why be limited to monotonous poured concrete, or even brick? Given the range of options in ceramic, stone, and concrete tiles, it's easy to create entirely fresh effects with a tiled patio or walk. Envision a winding, tiled path to a quiet, tiled sitting alcove. Or try an integrated patio with handpainted decorative tile on borders, stair risers, and a central fountain. Or plan a tiled interior landing that flows through French doors and out into the garden.

You will need to plan carefully. In cold climates, your tile choice must

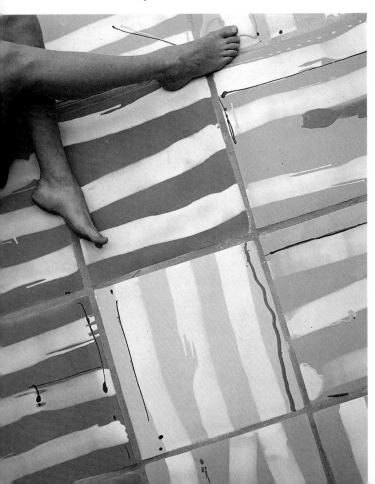

DESIGN: BENEDIKT STREBEL CERAMICS

be freeze-thaw stable. Impervious and vitreous options, including stone, unglazed porcelain, and quarry tiles, are your best choices for cooler outdoor environments. In milder climates, terra-cotta creates an ambience of earthy charm.

Patio tile must also be slip resistant. Matte, sandblasted, and "split" surfaces are workable options. Pavers, glazed tiles, and mosaics now come with abrasive additives for safer footing. Save handpainted or glossy, glazed tiles for small, occasional accents where their lack of traction won't matter. Penetrating sealers can protect soft, porous tiles from moisture and stains.

A tiled patio should be installed over a sturdy base of poured concrete, and in colder climates or unstable soils, over a subbase of crushed gravel. The paving should be sloped slightly away from the house or toward a drain. If you have a boring old backyard slab, you're actually in luck: the base for your new tile is already in place.

Water features. Tile makes a great pool surround or deck, provided it's thoroughly slip resistant. Pool steps, in particular, must offer sure footing. Here, unglazed mosaics and glazed tiles with abrasive additives are good choices. The pool edging, or coping, can also be tiled, though poured, tinted concrete is the trouble-free norm. The area just below water level is probably the best place for decorative tile work, such as colorful ceramics, art mosaics, or shimmering glass. Chlorine may react with some glazes, so it's best to consult with an experienced pool contractor before making your choices.

Spa floors, being smaller than pools, are better bets for an overall tile treatment; they're also easier to view. Stone, glass, and ceramic borders are great ways to link a spa and pool, both to each other and to the surrounding landscape.

You'll also see several ideas for decorative tiled wall fountains on the following pages. Go a traditional route with intricate Moorish patterns or formal

A glistening, glass-tiled spa face works handsomely with both brick and slate in this dramatic poolside setting.

stone, or get more playful with modern mosaics, glass, or—in mild climates— glazed wall tiles.

Entertainment areas. Barbecues, outdoor kitchens, wet bars, fireplaces, and conversation areas all benefit from easy-to-clean decorative tile. Plan here as you would for indoor uses, but be sure to take your climate into account. Don't use soft glazed wall tiles or other nonvitreous types where snow flies.

Tough tiles are especially suitable for countertops on outdoor kitchens and serving tables—they can stand up to both repeated storms and repeated cleanings. And, of course, there's no rule against tiling the top of a patio table or bench.

Beds and borders. In landscaping, the use of edgings—the defining trim along garden beds—helps tie together elements of a unified scheme. Why not build them from tile? A tiled garden edging serves the same decorative role as interior borders and moldings, while doing duty as walkway curb, raised-bed edge, or mowing-strip boundary. The tile pattern can restate or play off some tile accent in patio, fountain, or exterior trim. For an even more cohesive look, you can tile a freestanding planter or container to match. Either decorate an existing container or make your own from exterior-grade plywood.

Wall art. Walls are traditional garden focal points and offer dramatic expanses for a tile mural, a geometric pattern, or an abstract art mosaic. What about a delicately tiled wall niche? Or a cheery, quaint window box?

Don't overlook the opportunity to work tile into a house façade in the form of window trim, door trim, or random patterns of art tiles along wood siding or embedded in stucco. Tiled street numerals, fence accents, and gate designs individualize the approach from the street to your home.

Slick tiles can be trouble outdoors, but some new glazed floor tiles are toothy enough for safe footing on the veranda. And while they resemble both stone and terra-cotta, they're easier to maintain than either.

Inlaid tiles add pattern and texture to the smooth contours of this outdoor stucco fireplace in a Houston courtyard.

LANDSCAPE DESIGN: DAVID SAMUELSON, MCDUGALD-STEELE LANDSCAPE ARCHITECTS

A beautifully crafted stone mosaic forms a decorative "doormat" on a second-story porch; it's surrounded by large squares of limestone tile.

DESIGN: MONTEGIORDANO MOSAICS

LANDSCAPE ARCHITECT: JEFF STONE ASSOCIATES OF LA JOLLA

A tiny backyard in a housing-development condo uses saltillo pavers laid atop an old concrete slab. The tiles are grouted with gray mortar and blend with natural flagstones and river rocks.

Alternating glazed risers of cobalt blue and playful striped waves are topped with nonslip terra-cotta treads in this outdoor stairway.

LANDSCAPE DESIGNER: PHIL SNOW

ARCHITECT: ROBERT WYLIE

*A collection of glazed Arts
and Crafts-style tiles was
the basis for this front-
porch remodel. The home-
owners laid a commemo-
rative tile for each person
who worked on the house.
These tiles get a bit slick,
so slip-resisting mats are
added in wet weather.*

*Multihued slate tile wraps
an outdoor entertainment
space, extending from the
huge patio squares over the
built-in barbecue and on
up the house wall. Note the
clean, contrasting borders
that trim both serving area
and wall corners.*

The pleasing pastels of tiled borders in pool and spa are repeated in intricate mosaic murals behind both fountain and serving counter, pulling this broad outdoor entertainment area together visually.

A water-blue patchwork of glazed tile glows in the playfully winding "creek" that meanders past brushed-concrete spaces to a tiled pond beyond.

TILE ARTISAN: TINA AYERS/GRAPHICS IN TILE. LANDSCAPE DESIGNER: PROSCAPE LANDSCAPE DESIGN. INTERIOR DESIGNER: THOMAS BARTLETT INTERIORS

Iridescent glass tiles dress a classic wall fountain; as twilight falls, fiber-optic strips embedded in glass borders glow and show the tiles' highlights.

TILE ARTISAN: TINA AYERS/GRAPHICS IN TILE

A tiled water feature
doubles as both spa and
garden pool. Neutral
terra-cotta pavers form
a background for intensely
colored patterns
and borders.

*More than 20 shades
of blue, purple, and green
tiles, set in concentric circles,
lend new drama to what
was once a worn-out,
white-plastered pool. The
tiles range in size from
1 to 8 inches square.*

great tile ideas

This enclosed front garden's retaining wall features a great view: it's a tiled wall mural. The framed scene is a colorful rendering of a fondly remembered Hawaiian beach.

TILE ARTISAN: MARLO BARTELS STUDIO OF LAGUNA BEACH

Tiny ceramic shards add up to form bold, geometric shapes that serve as a dramatic backdrop for this swimming pool. They're weather-tight, too.

TILE ARTISAN: DEBRA YATES. LANDSCAPE ARCHITECT: RAYMOND JUNGLES

A collection of antique
Tunisian tiles seems right
at home as a decorative
outdoor wainscot.

TILE ARTISAN: MARLO BARTELS STUDIO OF LAGUNA BEACH
MEDALLION DESIGN: MATT KENYON

Iridescent, interlocking
tiles join with cables and
half-round borders to
outline a set of exterior
French doors. Custom
relief-cast ceramic
medallions stud the trim
at regular junctures.

ARCHITECT: ROB WELLINGTON QUIGLEY. DESIGN: ENVIRONMENTAL DWELLINGS, INC.

A SHOPPER'S GUIDE

Colorful wall tiles, earthy floor tiles, dazzling art tiles, playful mosaics: with all the choices, it's hard not to feel both exhilarated and a little overwhelmed when stepping into a tile showroom or home center. And ceramic isn't the only game in town. Thanks to current technologies, stone can be a stunning—and newly affordable—tile choice, as can dramatic glass or tinted concrete. **This chapter** is meant to work in tandem with earlier chapters in the book, serving as a nuts-and-bolts resource to help you implement the ideas discussed in "A Planning Primer." Stimulated by the many colorful installations shown throughout the gallery sections and equipped with this basic technical vocabulary, you should feel comfortable exploring your options and making a final decision. **We've said** it before but we're saying it again: color, pattern, and texture are only part of the formula for success. The real key is to pick the material that's appropriate for your location. Think water resistance, slip resistance, durability, and ease of maintenance. For information that can help you evaluate different tiles in these respects, see page 14.

Glazed Wall Tiles

MIX AND MATCH FOR VIBRANT CONTRASTS AND PATTERNS

ARCHITECT: SUZAN NETTLESHIP. CONTRACTOR: IRIS HARRELL

Smaller, lighter, and thinner than floor tiles, most wall tiles are not meant to withstand either high heels or hot pots. But their lightness is a plus for vertical installation and for cutting, and they come in a dazzling array of colors and textures.

Commercial wall tiles are made by the dust-press method, and the machine-made precision of their shapes works especially well with the clean lines of many contemporary designs. They're usually set closely together, with thin (1/16-inch) grout lines—often calibrated via built-in lug spacers on the tiles' edges.

Although the white, gypsum-based tile bodies are generally nonvitreous (see page 14), the glazing process makes their faces (but not their edges or backs) both water and stain resistant. Water-resistant backing, adhesive, and grout (see page 29) can improve performance, but for vulnerable locations like showers, floors, and exteriors in

A creative mix of readily available wall tiles and borders echoes kitchen colors elsewhere and neatly ties the sleek hood and cooktop together.

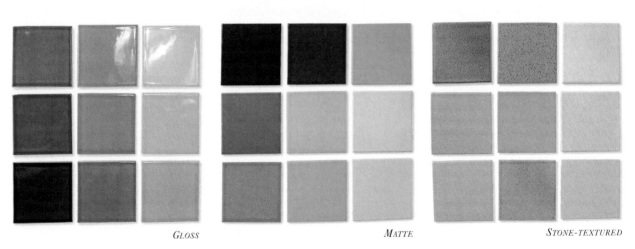

GLOSS *MATTE* *STONE-TEXTURED*

freezing climates, choose vitreous or impervious tiles.

Increasingly, the distinction between traditional wall tiles and art tiles (see pages 98–101) is blurring, as wall tiles take on both new colors and finishes.

Colors range from quiet whites and creams through soft pastels to glowing reds and deep, intense blues, and if you can't find what you want, your dealer can probably order custom colors. Surface finishes can be glossy, matte, or textured, and glazes can have a metallic, crackled, or brushed look instead of the customary flat color. For a sampling, see the photos below.

Most wall tiles have soft glazes, which are usually not a problem on tub surrounds or backsplashes. A few, with Mohs hardness ratings of 5 or higher, may be suitable for light-duty bathroom or bedroom floors (if they pass the slip-resistance test). In general, the shinier the glaze, the more easily it's scratched.

Some wall tiles are tough enough to be used as countertops. But check with the dealer to be sure the tile's surface can withstand both abrasion and chemicals (the acids in some foods, for example, can etch

Tile nippers help nibble cutouts and irregular shapes in wall tiles; you'll want them when tiling around sinks or plumbing fixtures.

through certain glazes, especially those with copper-based green pigment).

Common sizes for glazed wall tiles include 3 by 3, 4¹/₄ by 4¹/₄, and 6 by 6 inches; larger squares and rectangles

may also be available. These dimensions are nominal and may not be exactly accurate, so be sure to take precise measurements of the tiles you like. Nominal thickness is usually about ¹/₄ to ⁵/₁₆ inch.

Prices range from as little as 50 cents per commercial tile to $20 or more per square foot for custom colors or one-of-a-kind creations. Generally, the more tiles of a particular size, glaze, and ornamentation that are manufactured, the less each one will cost.

Remember that you can create complex designs from the most basic of tiles. Commercial wall tiles are easily cut to form variant units that work with basic squares. And because these tiles come in such a variety of colors, they can be mixed and matched to create endless contrasts and custom-look patterns.

Many wall tile lines include coordinated border and trim pieces (for additional details, see pages 104–105). Some integrated lines include matching floor tiles, countertop tiles, and coordinated bathroom fixtures. Some even offer matching ceramic soap dishes, towel bars, and other accessories.

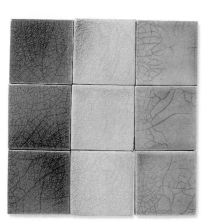

CRACKLED

METALLIC

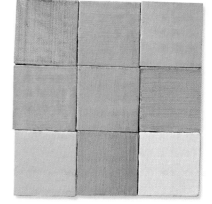

BRUSHED

Floor Tiles

GLAZED OR UNGLAZED, THEY'RE TOUGH ENOUGH FOR HEAVY TRAFFIC

Compared to wall tiles, floor tiles are larger, thicker, and more durable. You don't want to use wall tiles on floors, but many floor tiles can also be suitable for countertops and walls.

Floor tiles come glazed or unglazed. Unglazed tiles are generally less slippery and don't show wear as much since their coloration extends throughout the clay body. They are, however, more subject to staining.

Precise terms for floor tiles are hard to corral, as descriptive terms like "paver," "glazed," and "handmade" seem to have different meanings in different locales, and even on opposite sides of the dealer's aisle! With that said, there are basically four types you're likely to encounter: quarry tiles, porcelain pavers, glazed floor tiles, and terra-cotta tiles—each distinguished by its composition and method of manufacture.

PORCELAIN PAVERS

Quarry tiles

These sturdy tiles are made by the extrusion process—you can usually identify them by roller grooves on their backs. Though some quarry tiles are glazed, most come unglazed in natural clay colors of yellow, brown, rust, or red. Some exhibit "flashing," heat-produced shadings that vary from tile to tile. Most quarry tiles are vitreous, making them hardworking and stable outdoors.

Typical sizes are 6 by 6, 8 by 8, and 12 by 12 inches. You'll also find 3 by 6 and 4 by 8 rectangles and a smattering of hexagons. Nominal thickness varies from about 3/8 to 3/4 inch.

Though the manufacturing process produces a tough surface that helps ward off stains, unglazed quarry tiles can be sealed to increase stain resistance in heavy-traffic areas.

Porcelain pavers

The best porcelain is highly refined clay that's dust-pressed and fired at more than 2000°F to form a dense body classified as impervious or vitreous. The waterproof, stain-resistant nature of these tiles makes them great choices for heavy-traffic areas indoors and, if slip resistant, for outdoor patios and walkways.

Porcelain pavers frequently resemble slate, limestone, and other stones, but come in pastel colors, too. While many tiles are polished, more slip-resistant textures include "split" (resembling slate), "sandblasted," and various embossed surfaces with raised grids.

Though 12- by 12-inch pavers are standard, sizes range from 4- by 6-inch rectangles up through 24- by 24-inch Italian *monocottura* (single-fired) squares.

NOTCHED TROWEL

QUARRY TILES

Glazed floor tiles

Though they're also called "pavers," the important thing to remember about floor tiles termed "ceramic" or "glazed" is that they're made of high-fired, dust-pressed clay that becomes vitreous or semivitreous. Unlike the extrusion grooves on a quarry tile, raised dots or grids appear on the backs of these.

Of course, there are glazed tiles for walls as well as floors, but floor tiles generally have much tougher glazes. These tiles are often rated for durability: for a heavy-traffic area, choose a tile with an Abrasive Wear Index rating of 3 or higher and a Mohs hardness rating of 7 or 8.

Typical sizes are 8 by 8 and 12 by 12 inches. Nominal thickness is about $5/16$ inch.

Some glazed floor tiles have textured or matte surfaces for better traction and longer wear. They're also increasingly available in stonelike textures and finishes built up from multilayer glazes, some looking remarkably like the real thing. Special nonslip tiles have abrasive additives in their glazes. Still, some experts say, "If it's glazed, don't use it in wet areas."

GLAZED FLOOR TILES

Terra-cotta

Translated from the Italian, *terra-cotta* means "cooked earth." But whether you see terra-cotta in antique French folk tile, hand-formed Mexican slabs, or rustic Italian or Portuguese wares, the charm of this material lies in its very lack of consistency. Unless tiles have been whitewashed or stained, the surface color goes all the way through the clay. Terra-cotta tiles come as squares, rectangles, hexagons, and octagons, as well as in Moorish, ogee, and other interlocking shapes.

Terra-cotta tiles are nonvitreous and highly absorbent, and so are questionable for outdoor use in freezing climates. They also need to be sealed (see facing page) for protection against surface water and stains. Some quarry tiles mimic the look of terra-cotta (though without its quirky charm) and can substitute for it in high-traffic or wet areas.

Saltillo tiles (named for the area in Mexico where they are made) are especially popular in the Southwest and West, where their rugged, earth-toned honesty seems culturally at home. Here, the clay is hand-packed into wooden or metal frames, set in the sun to dry, then given a low-temperature firing. Lime holes or "pops," dinged corners, variations in size and thickness, color differences from firing—all these variables lend a homey individuality to their look. So-called "super saltillos" have rounded edges that help reduce chipping.

HEXAGONS WITH GLAZED DOTS

TERRA-COTTA TILES

ANTIQUE FRENCH PAVERS

TO SEAL OR NOT TO SEAL?

In most cases, you needn't seal a floor tile that's glazed. Most impervious and vitreous tiles don't need sealing, either. The prime candidates for sealers are unglazed terra-cotta and some quarry tiles.

In the past, terra-cotta tiles were finished with built-up layers of beeswax or similar coatings which, over time, produced a leatherlike patina. Modern sealers break down into surface and penetrating types.

Surface or top sealers offer more resistance to stains but darken tiles and produce a sheen that may or may not be appealing; they also must be stripped and reapplied periodically.

Penetrating sealers soak into the tile instead of coating its surface. But they're not as protective as top sealers.

Some floor tiles, such as saltillos, are available presealed; others must be sealed on site. Unless you've used an epoxy grout (see page 29), the grout lines may need sealing as well. In this case, grout is often sealed at the same time as the tiles. While it's possible to "paint" sealer onto grout spaces only, this is an extremely tedious process.

Because it's unwise to use toxic sealers around food, most tile experts warn against choosing countertop tiles that require resealing. Some quarry tiles can give you the earthy look of terra-cotta in your kitchen without the sealer danger and maintenance problems. Sealer technology is changing all the time, and some proprietary formulas vary from region to region. What's the lesson? Always explain your installation and ask a knowledgeable dealer for specifics. And be sure to inquire about maintenance requirements.

Whatever sealer you select, it's best to test its appearance on a sample tile before applying it to your floor.

A stacked pair of saltillo tiles shows the contrast between an unsealed unit (top) *and the shiny, presealed version* (bottom).

Art Tiles

TAKE YOUR PICK: FAITHFUL PERIOD PIECES OR BOLD, MODERN DESIGNS

Much of the energy of today's tile renaissance comes from the recent explosion of interest in decorative art tiles, both original designs and recreations of traditional styles.

Aside from its visual and tactile appeal, tile can be a powerful way to allude to period or regional styles, and in this respect a few art tiles or a handpainted mural can go a long way toward setting the decorative tone for an entire room. You can choose handmade tiles with softly irregular shapes to create folk or historical allusions, or crisp, machine-made patterns to support a high-tech contemporary look. The gamut runs from charmingly pictorial to dynamically abstract designs.

A rainbow of options

Some art tiles are faithful reproductions of traditional Arts and Crafts, Victorian, or Moorish-inspired designs; others create more exuberant looks that respectfully acknowledge their ancestors but make fresh departures. Still others strike out to create bold, contemporary graphics. A cross section of styles is shown on these pages.

Decorative tiles are generally nonvitreous like glazed wall tiles. Many have glazes that are easily scratched. Traditionally, they've clad fireplace surrounds, stair risers, courtyard fountains, even patio walls in temperate climates. Modern uses include service as kitchen and bath backsplashes, vent hoods, window trim, tub surrounds, and walk-in showers.

Though some art tiles can be used as floor accents, most (with the notable exceptions of encaustic tiles and some decorative terra-cotta) are not meant to handle foot traffic.

The tiles shown here and on the facing page give a glimpse of your options, including both hand- and machine-formed tiles decorated in styles from naturalistic to abstract.

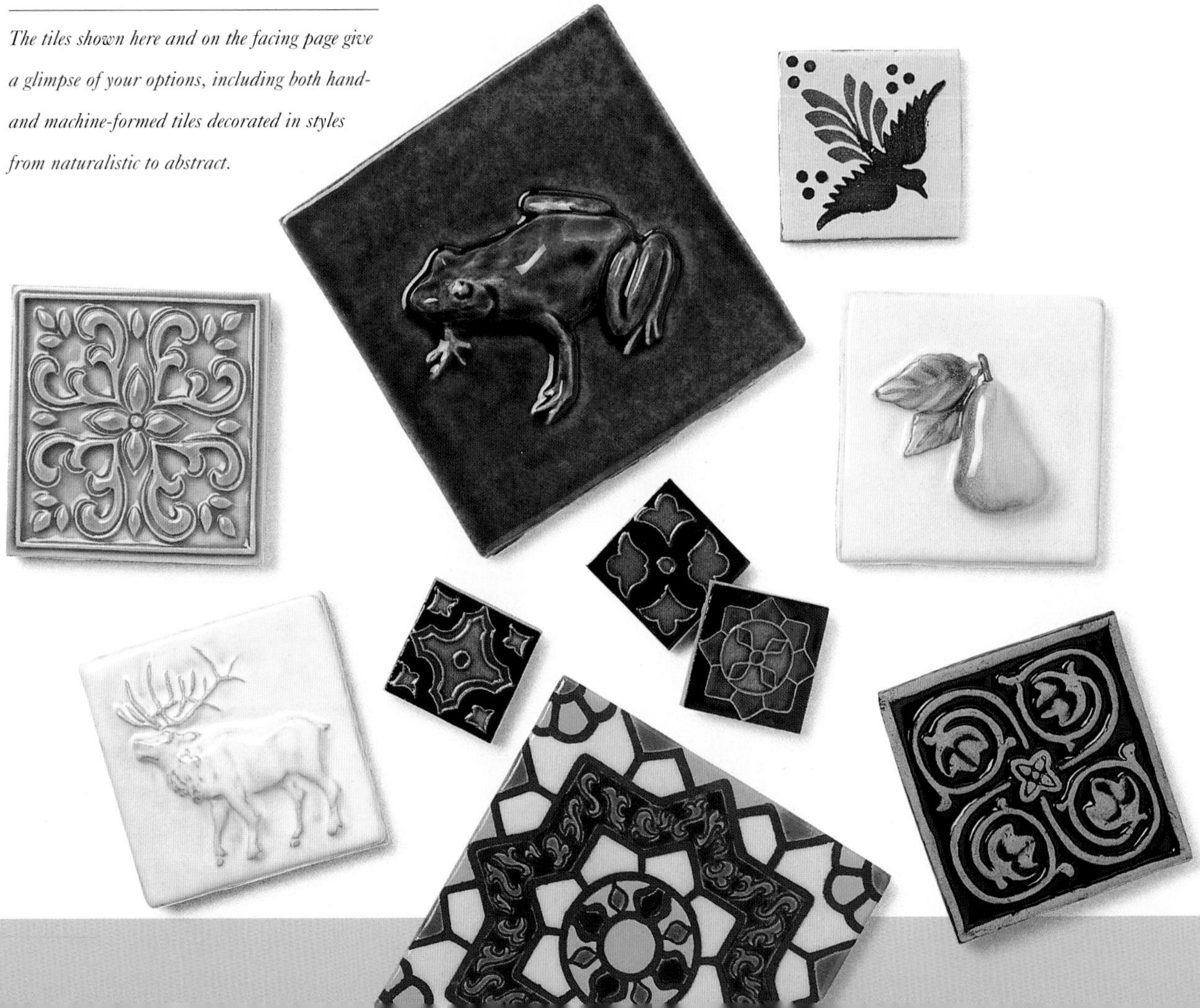

Some historic patterns were created from linoleum-block carvings impressed in the clay. Others used wax-based resist lines as barriers between glazes in different colors.

Today, some manufacturers mold their tiles by hand, but others machine-press the clay. Handmade tiles are usually more prized than machined tiles, with "relaxed" shapes and rounded corners, plus variations in size and thickness. These idiosyncrasies,

signs of the individuality of the artisan's hand, are part of such tiles' appeal.

Whether the clay body is formed by hand or machine, the depths and nuances of some art tile glazes are nothing short of magic. Glazing formulas and firing times and temperatures are closely guarded secrets; some art tiles may be glazed and refired eight or nine times. ´

Handpainted tiles are typically decorated in a labor-intensive fashion,

with small brushes used to apply the color. Other patterns are silk-screened. Some makers use multiple layers and multiple firings to build colors, and others separate them by using wax borders. Less expensive offerings may use applied decals instead.

Art tiles with raised profiles are termed *relief* tiles; those with indentations are called *counter-relief*. Sturdy *encaustic* tiles, used since the days of England's great cathedrals, fill this recess with a contrasting color of liquid clay, called a *slip*.

Most art tile producers are small operations, making their tiles to order. However, larger manufacturers are jumping on the bandwagon, offering a growing variety of art-look machine-made tiles and borders.

Elegant art tile textures include an etched-copper patina (below, top), *glossy relief pattern with matching borders* (below, bottom), *and a traditional encaustic design with contrasting clays* (below, right).

Decorative murals

Tile murals come in two basic types: individual "sheet" murals and large scenes built up from numerous individual tiles. Many murals in showrooms are coordinated with plain field tiles, and some lines also offer border tiles and corner trim.

Most traditional tile murals are built up from numerous individual tiles, handpainted or silk-screened as one, then separated, numbered, and reassembled. Perennial motifs include floral bouquets, fruits and vegetables, animals, and nature scenes. But there's no reason to stop with such subjects: tile showrooms often work with local artisans to custom-design handpainted murals. Treatments can be conservative to whimsical to wild!

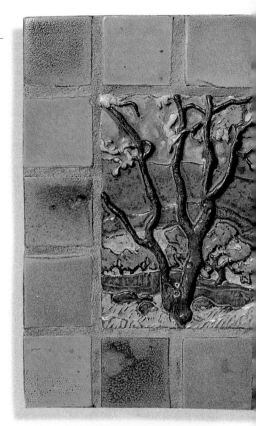

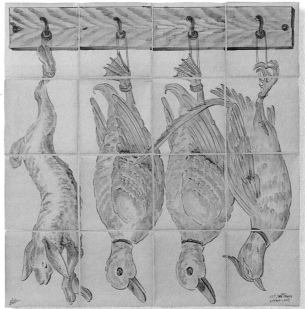

The decorative Arts and Crafts mural (above, left) *is all of a piece. Handpainted Portuguese tiles* (above) *and sunflowers* (left) *are assembled from prematched, individual tiles. A photo-mural* (below) *pairs a light-sensitive emulsion layer with a protective top glaze.*

Ceramic Mosaics

SHOP FOR PREMOUNTED PATTERNS OR ONE-OF-A-KIND ARTWORKS

Ceramic mosaics are among the most colorful and versatile materials in the tile family. Mosaic tiles look striking on floors and walls, and the smaller ones can wrap around columns or follow the contours of garden walls and swimming pools.

Mosaics come either as premounted, factory-made patterns or as one-of-a-kind, free-form artworks designed and built from scratch.

Manufactured mosaics

When it comes to commercial products, the term "mosaic" means any very small tile from $3/4$ by $3/4$ inch up to about 2 by 2 inches. Shapes include squares, rectangles, octagons, hexagons, and special designs.

These small tiles are mounted together on a common backing in larger sections—typically 12 by 12 inches or 12 by 24 inches—and in numerous patterns and grids (grout spacings are included). Backings may be nylon, plastic, or paper; several are shown at right. Most mosaics are meant to be aligned with adjacent panels, then simply pressed into adhesive and grouted when dry. Some, however, are front-mounted: the paper is sponged or peeled away once the adhesive sets.

Mosaics can be of natural clay tile or hard porcelain and are available both glazed and unglazed. Scratch-resistant, unglazed versions are best for floors and countertops; in these,

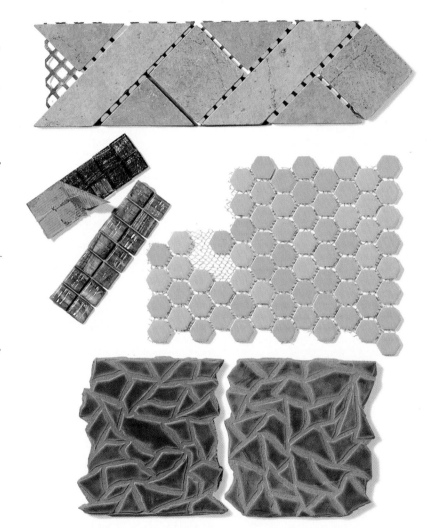

Premounted products range from tried-and-true squares and octagons to broken shapes that mimic the look of free-form art mosaics. Backings include nylon, plastic, and paper.

the color is integrated with the wet bisque. Most mosaics are either impervious or vitreous. This, plus the natural slip resistance provided by myriad grout joints, makes them excellent choices for water-susceptible locations in bathrooms and kitchens and outdoors. Some mosaics contain a nonslip additive for additional safety.

Because of the new-found popularity of free-form or "art" mosaics, you can often order custom designs and decorations premounted at the factory. You may also wish to take a look at mosaics made from stone (see page 109) and glass (page 110).

RUBBER FLOAT

Art mosaics

The one-of-a-kind look of free-form design is partly responsible for the current enthusiasm for mosaics and for art tiles in general. Some mosaic works are collages of found materials that might blend bits of smashed tile, shards of pottery or table china, broken glass, pebbles, even marbles. The look can be representational or gleefully abstract.

Most art mosaics are very labor-intensive, so they tend to be expensive. Some are first laid out in factory or studio, mounted on backing sections, moved to the site, and installed. Others are done completely on-site. Dissimilar materials are "floated" to varying depths in a thick layer of "mud" (mortar); the mortar becomes an integral part of the design.

These two mosaics have the look of one-of-a-kind artworks but can be ordered through a tile showroom. The playful swirls (top) leave plenty of space for contrasting grout, making it an integral part of the pattern. The twin trout (left) are swimming through a mosaic that artfully follows their contours, not those of randomly smashed pieces.

Borders & Trim

FINISHING TOUCHES FROM ROPES TO LINERS TO BULLNOSES

Both borders and trim tiles accent and finish off installations of field tiles, particularly on walls and countertops. What's the difference? Borders set off transitions between spaces or between materials and draw the eye to highlighted areas. Offerings include relief tiles, handpainted tiles, and other treatments borrowed from art tiles. Trim tiles, however, are made to blend in with field tiles and finish off the open edges, ends, and corners of those installations.

Many commercial wall tiles come with corresponding trim and coordinated borders. When you're considering a field tile, take a look at these options. Or check borders that match a similar line but work effectively with your selection.

Borders and more borders

Relief-tile borders can be boldly playful or quietly monochromatic, adding the visual interest of contrasting texture with or without contrasting color.

A selection of shapes and styles is shown on the facing page. Typically, border tiles are more expensive than field tiles.

Most border tiles come in small sections, typically 6 inches long, and are meant to be lined up and grouted like field tiles. Usually, they're staggered so that grout spaces offset field tiles—otherwise, they'd probably be at least a distracting hair off.

Some border tiles double as trim tiles—for example, those used at the top of a wainscot or chair rail. You'll also find ceramic versions of traditional wood moldings, including profiles for base, crown, and chair rail uses.

Trim tiles

Unlike border tiles, which are primarily decorative, trim tiles are designed to finish off the raw or cut edges of wall or countertop tiles, which are typically unglazed or uncolored.

Trim tiles come in two basic families: surface and radius. Common profiles include bullnose (rounded edge),

Utilitarian trim tiles (left) *finish off raw edges, ends, and corners; borders* (facing page) *are unabashedly decorative.*

TILE ACCESSORIES

Some wall tiles have matching glazed ceramic accessories—soap dishes, towel bars, and glass and toothbrush holders. Accessories are usually laid out in advance and installed and grouted along with field tiles; otherwise, a space is left and they're added after the field tiles set up.

If your tile choice has no accessories—or if you don't like the options—you can either pick a complementary line's accessories or simply down-play their need by building in tiled shelves, niches, and towel hooks as you go.

Remember that numerous lines of commercial tile come in integrated lines that coordinate with bathroom and kitchen fixtures as well as trim and accessories. You can even find beautiful handpainted sinks that match handsome art tiles—though often at a handsome price, too.

down-angle (two rounded edges), cove, quarter-round, half-round, V cap, end cap, and sink corner.

Surface trim completes the edges and corners where field tiles were applied directly to a flat wall or countertop surface. It's generally only the thickness of a standard tile. *Radius* trim takes a bigger bend to cover the exposed edge of the substrate below—as when a wainscot of concrete backerboard ends halfway up a wall. Radius trim is also used at the front edge of a countertop to provide a thicker, more substantial bullnose than surface trim would.

What if the field tile you like doesn't come with trim? Look for a complementary trim in another line; miter (cut) field tiles to turn corners; or opt for unglazed field tiles that have consistent color on their edges and cut surfaces. Tiles with integral color can also be honed or ground to form a bevel or curve.

Stone Tiles

NEW TECHNIQUES MAKE THEM BEAUTIFUL, PRACTICAL, AND AFFORDABLE

STONE TILES AND TRIM

New diamond-saw techniques have made stone tiles, once a luxury, competitive in price with quality ceramic products. Consider stone anywhere you'd use ceramic—for example, on entry floors, patios, kitchen countertops, bathroom wainscots, and backsplashes. Though some natural stone absorbs water and stains readily, new sealers (see pages 108–109) are improving resistance.

Stone tile is installed in a similar manner to ceramic, though variations in size, thickness, and strength can make it a little trickier to work with. When shopping, remember that these tiles are natural, one-of-a-kind products, and be sure to order extra—you can't match them later.

Stone types

Natural stone falls into one of three general categories: igneous, sedimentary, or metamorphic. *Igneous* rock is hardest, being formed from molten material below the earth's surface under tremendous heat and pressure. *Sedimentary* stones are softest, as they consist of stratified layers of ancient marine or sand deposits. *Metamorphic* rocks are sedimentary in origin, but have undergone changes from heat and pressure that have made them tougher—and sometimes more brittle.

■ **GRANITE** is a hard, close-grained igneous rock that comes in hues from salt-and-pepper gray through rich rust tones to black. Granite is the densest of stone tiles, the equivalent of vitreous ceramic in wear and water resistance. Though costly, it's popular—and appropriate—for tub surrounds, walk-in showers, and countertops.

■ **MARBLE,** an elegant metamorphic rock, offers tremendous variety in color and veining, but is somewhat softer and weaker than granite and more susceptible to stains. It should be sealed when used in wet areas.

■ **LIMESTONE,** usually creamy white to soft gold-beige, is a sedimentary rock that's gaining in popularity as new sealers come on the market. More porous than either granite or marble, limestone must be sealed to prevent unsightly staining.

■ **SLATE** is a traditional, metamorphic choice that tends to split along natural grains and fissures, producing a rustic surface that's appropriate indoors and out. It can also be polished or honed like marble.

■ **TRAVERTINE** is a limestone that's formed near underground springs. Its natural pits may collect grout when installed, and water later; for wet areas, consider a "filled" version.

■ **ONYX** sports rich, swirling amber pockets and quartz veining. Too temperamental and pricey for some applications, it's often reserved for showy but low-maintenance areas.

■ **QUARTZITE** is a pebbly metamorphic rock that's formed from sandstone. Less common than other stone options for tile, quartzite is tough as well as good-looking.

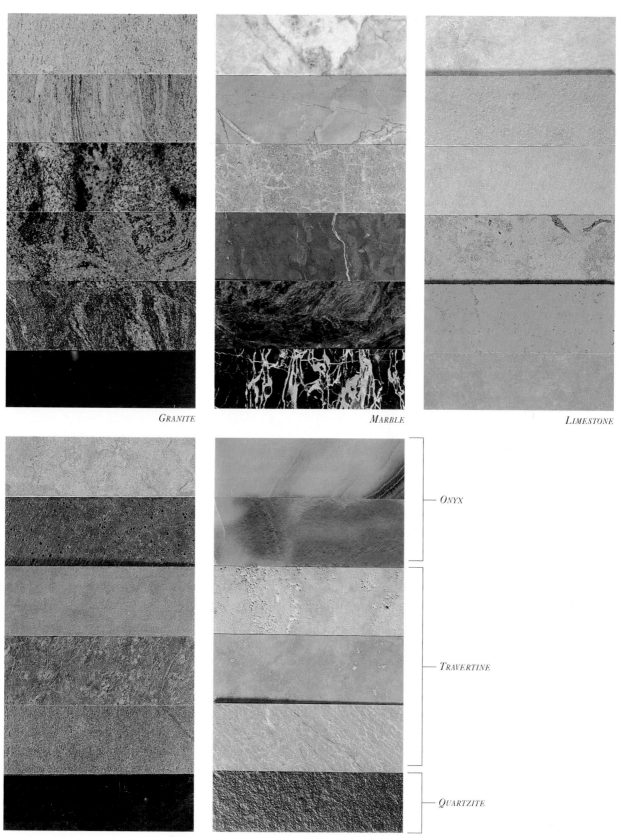

GRANITE

MARBLE

LIMESTONE

ONYX

TRAVERTINE

QUARTZITE

SLATE

Popular stone textures (shown above counter-clockwise, from bottom to top) *include polished, honed, tumbled, sandblasted, resplit, and flamed. A striking laser-jet inlay is shown below.*

Honing is like reverse polishing—producing a surface that is smooth but less shiny and slippery than that of polished stone.

The popular *tumbled* finish is produced by jostling marble tiles in a machine until they take on a rounded, chalky, antiqued look.

Resplit tiles show a cleft, craggy face; *flamed* surfaces are craggy but rounded; and *sandblasted* tiles have a uniform, pebbly surface.

In addition, you'll also find *resawn* faces—a rougher, slip-resistant variation of honed tiles that plainly shows the circular path of the diamond-tipped saw blade.

Chemical treatments include intentional etching (with a muriatic acid solution) which produces dramatic effects, and color enhancing which highlights or darkens stone colors and grains.

Laser-jet technology has made it possible to design and produce striking "inlay" pictures and patterns such as the one shown below left.

What about sealers?

Like porous ceramic tiles, those made from soft stones, such as marble, need to be sealed against staining and acid damage.

At the very least—and even if you don't mind a little patina—you should apply a stone soap. If you seal with a stone soap, use the same product for routine cleaning.

To better resist surface staining and etching, apply a penetrating sealer and then a hard wax, such as carnauba wax, or a newer natural-synthetic blend. This treatment will buy you some time to clean up spills that could etch through the wax and into the stone.

New textures, new technologies

Polished marble is the traditional, elegant option for a formal entryway or living room. And although polished surfaces tend to dull and show wear most easily, they can be repolished by professionals.

Other, rougher textures have recently been gaining prominence—partly for their slip resistance, but also for easier maintenance and for the matte, pastel looks they can produce. Several treatments are shown above—including honing, tumbling, flaming, sandblasting, and resplitting.

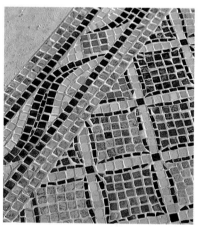

A stone mosaic panel (left) *is shown atop its integral backing; an installed version* (below), *featuring tumbled stones, livens up a doorway threshold. Colorful terrazzo tile* (bottom left) *is now available in standard 12-inch sizes.*

New surface coatings that will virtually block stains and etching are being developed, but they're expensive and labor-intensive. Since these new products are both locally based and constantly changing, the best approach is to discuss your specific needs with a knowledgeable stone supplier.

Terrazzo

Known as a manufactured stone or *agglomerate*, terrazzo tile is typically made by setting chips of marble or onyx in concrete and then polishing the surface. Although commonly produced in large slabs, terrazzo is also available in 12- by 12-inch tiles that

can be installed like stone or ceramic. Usually terrazzos don't have the toughness or color retention of true stone; but they're admirable recycled products, and newer versions are constantly improving in durability.

Stone mosaics

The tradition of stone mosaics is undergoing a rebirth. Just as with ceramic mosaics (see pages 102–103), stone mosaics come in two types: the premounted composition on backing, and the custom art piece put together from scratch in a studio or on-site.

Stone showrooms can help you select and custom-order a mosaic that's made in a factory or studio, mounted on manageable sections that are numbered in sequence and can be reassembled and grouted on-site.

Other Options

Glass and concrete are examples of familiar materials that are being used in bold, new ways, including as tile.

Tile dealers and masonry suppliers may have other products as well. When faced with any new tile material, ask the same questions you'd ask of ceramic. Is it durable? Will it stain easily? Will it stand up to moisture or frost?

Glass

Artistic glass has, of course, been around for centuries, but not in the many tile forms now available. Glass tiles come in many colors, from primaries to pastels—some transparent, some smoked, some opaque. Surfaces may be super-smooth or craggy. Some tiles have graceful relief designs; others have shimmering, iridescent glazes; still others are handpainted. Many offerings are eco-friendly, consisting mainly of recycled materials.

Most glass tiles are impervious to moisture, making them useful inside and out for decorative floors (if slip resistant), backsplashes, tub and shower surrounds, and swimming pools or wall fountains.

Typically, glass tiles are installed much like ceramic tiles, and are trimmed as required with a wet saw and diamond blade. Most installers

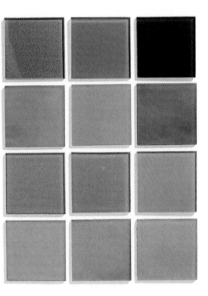

Glass, whether in the form of mosaics (top left), *wall tiles* (top right), *or art tiles and borders* (right), *offers dramatic decorative possibilities.*

choose special adhesive and grout when working with clear or translucent tiles.

Glass mosaics, like ceramic ones (see pages 102–103), are built up from small pieces (typically 1 by 1 inch) that are premounted on paper sheets. They're sometimes called *Venetian* glass when made from regular shapes.

Concrete

The news is out: concrete is undergoing a radical transformation. The drab, utilitarian gray stuff is gaining both muted and vivid color palettes and appearing in interesting, surprising textures and bold forms—including tile. This wonderfully tactile material can be made as slick and shiny as a mirror or as rough-textured and non-reflecting as sandpaper.

The new spectrum gives homeowners exciting opportunities for combining textures and patterns, and far more choices when coordinating a concrete surface with other colors and materials in a room.

Concrete tiles make durable floors, walls, and wainscots and, if carefully installed, are suitable for wet areas. The range of shapes and sizes follows that of ceramic tile (including the ubiquitous 12-inch floor tiles). Most new tiles are made to order by custom concrete fabricators.

Concrete contains natural materials—stone, silica-based cement, and water. Like stone (but unlike synthetic products), concrete requires careful maintenance (see pages 108–109) and even when properly sealed can develop a patina from wear over time.

Concrete takes on new life in the colors and textures of these custom tiles; with proper care, they go anywhere that ceramic or stone can.

index

Photographers:
Unless noted, all photographs are by **Philip Harvey.**

Jean Allsopp: 30. **Alexis Andrews:** 61 bottom. **Peter Christiansen:** 72. **Christopher Irion:** 87. **Muffy Kibby:** 39 top. **David Duncan Livingston:** 32 bottom; 44 bottom; 61 top. **Sylvia Martin:** 50, 78. **Emily Minton:** 1, 35, 38, 40 top, 49, back cover top. **Norman Plate:** 81. **Lanny Provo:** 88 bottom. **Richard Ross:** 76 bottom. **Alan Weintraub:** 22. **Russ Widstrand:** 33. **Tom Wyatt:** 9 top; 92 top.

Photo credits/product shots:
ASN Natural Stone: 106–107 all; 108 top and bottom; 109 top. **Country Floors:** 17 top right; 18 top left; 26 right; 32 top; 96 top right; 97 top left; 101 top right; 105 right. **Rodger Dunham Ceramic Design of Petaluma:** 31. **Fireclay Tile:** 7; 13; 16; 17 lower right; 18 top center and bottom right; 62 top; 95 bottom; 96–97 bottom right; 97 far right; 98–99 all; 102 bottom. **Fireclay Tile/ Galleria Tile:** 3; 104; 105 left. **Galleria Tile:** 94; 95 top right; 96 bottom left; 102 top and center. **Galleria Tile/Tile Visions:** 109 bottom left; 110 top left. **Oceanside Glasstile:** 46 top; 110 bottom. **Osburn Design/ASN Natural Stone:** 27; 109 right. **Laird Plumleigh/Alchemie Ceramic Studio:** 15 top; 17 center right; 76 top; 100–101 center top. **Buddy Rhodes Studio:** 111. **Ann Sacks Tile & Stone:** 4 top; 9 bottom; 15 bottom; 17 bottom right; 18 bottom center; 19 bottom left and bottom right; 92 bottom; 93 bottom; 100 top left and bottom right; 103 top left and bottom left; 110 top right. **Diane Swift:** 8 top left; 26 top left; 100 bottom left; 101 bottom right. **Tile Visions:** 101 bottom left.

Boldface numbers refer to photographs